T0044825

PRIVATE LESSONS

THE MUSICIAN'S GUIDE TO
RECORDING
Vocals

by Dallan Beck

ALSO BY DALLAN BECK:
The Musician's Guide to Recording Acoustic Guitar (book/CD)
Home Recording Basics (video)

ISBN 0-634-02944-4

7777 W. BLUEMOUND RD. P.O. BOX 13819 MILWAUKEE, WI 53213

Visit Hal Leonard Online at
www.halleonard.com

TABLE OF CONTENTS

INTRODUCTION 4

GENERAL ADVICE 5

1   MICROPHONES 6

2   MIC PLACEMENT 11

3   COMPRESSION 18

4   EQUALIZATION 27

5   TRACKING VOCALS 31

6   EFFECTS 40

CLOSING & ACKNOWLEDGMENTS 51

CD INDEX 52

ANSWERS TO QUIZ QUESTIONS 54

Introduction

When I began writing and recording this book, my original intention was to use the SSL or Neve Studios at Musicians Institute in Los Angeles, California. This is where I currently record and teach, and where, on any given day, you could walk in and hear an album being recorded or mixed for any number of professional artists—from rock to pop to blues to fusion. If you haven't seen either of these two studios, they are beyond words: Each is outfitted with over one million dollars worth of recording equipment. And this has become a normal recording situation for me! (Hey, it took me ten long years to gain access to such high-end equipment—why would I use anything else?)

However, I soon began to wonder whether it would be fair to make a book/CD using this gear. Would it be productive for the average reader/listener? What was my goal in writing the book: To impress readers? To overwhelm them with unrealistic expectations? Or to give them a goal they could actually attain?

Of course, it was the latter. So I chose to put myself in your shoes. I built my own project studio, took all of the knowledge I could, and applied it to a setting that you might be using right now. I wanted this book/CD to be a text you could actually use, not just look at and listen to. I decided to step back and remember when I first started recording, and wished someone would've helped point me in the right direction. Where was that book that showed me actual examples, good and bad? Where was that book that gave me great new ideas or reminded me of old ideas that I had possibly overlooked?

So here it is: a basic guide to recording vocals. I hope it's valuable to you now, because it would've been valuable to me ten years ago. And when you master everything in this book, well, then it might be time for you to come down and see me at the Recording Institute of Technology.

Author in his home studio

General Advice

Before we delve into the fine details of capturing a vocal performance, let's get the basics down. To start with, there are four general ideas I'd like you to consider:

Idea 1: *Vocals are the most intimate of all instruments.*

Think about it, the voice is the only instrument we're born with, and therefore, it's the most personal and varied instrument in existence. The object of recording a vocal is to retain the unique and musical character inherent to the singer. We can enhance it, alter it, and mold it, but everything begins with the voice itself.

Before you do anything else, really listen to the singer's voice. Notice every detail, no matter how small or unimportant it might seem.

Idea 2: *When recording any instrument, there are three roles to be filled: the musician, the engineer, and the producer.*

The musician, in this case, is the singer. The engineer handles the technical side of capturing the performance while recording. The producer is the overall ears of what's going on. You might be doing all three by yourself, or there might be different people for each role. Just remember that all three inputs are important for creating a great recording experience. Sometimes the vocalist can't see the big picture of how everything connects in the song. Sometimes the engineer is too wrapped up in gear to notice what's going on emotionally in the song. The producer is supposed to mediate between the two, and also see the big picture or end result. (It's a lot of power being the producer, and everyone seems to want it. The question is, who's going to take responsibility for it?)

It's good for the engineer to have a basic understanding of singing; this helps the singer and engineer to communicate freely. If you are acting as both, you need to separate where the singer ends and the engineer begins.

Idea 3: *Find a reference CD.*

In order to produce a quality recording, I recommend using reference CDs. A reference CD is a recording on which you like the overall sounds. It sounds good to you everywhere you play it. In regards to vocals, the vocal level sounds right to you, no matter what type of system you listen on.

Most styles of music have a vocal level that's clearly heard apart from the music; some have it more blended in. When it comes time to mixing the vocals in the song, listen to your reference CD and make sure that your vocal levels are about the same. This will help insure that when you leave the studio, your vocals will not radically change from one stereo system to the next. There's nothing worse than thinking your vocals sound great, but then when the CD is played on your friend's system or at a party, they sound muddy or shrill or too thin.

Idea 4: *Be patient.*

Start with just miking up a singer and recording. Once you can hear that something's wrong with the vocals or the recording, then it's time to fix it. Too many students get caught up in using tons of gear, and they don't have a clue why. If you can't tell it's broken, don't fix it!

I'm going to give you many audio examples of what not to do in hopes that you can hear the problems as they arise. Knowledge comes to everyone at a different pace. Try to understand what you do and why you do it, and you'll have learned how to teach yourself.

Good luck!

Microphones

A microphone is a transducer—that is, something that converts one form of energy into another. In our case, sound waves are converted into electrical current.

Dynamic vs. Condenser

There are two types of microphones that you should be aware of as a consumer. The first are *dynamic* mics. Dynamic microphones are based on a magnetic principle to convert sound to electrical current. They do this through the use of a moving coil. In simple terms, the louder the input signal, the more the coil moves, the more sound/electrical current is transferred through the microphone. Because of this, dynamic mics handle loud, transient sounds very well. They're also good for rejecting feedback (from monitors), which makes them great for live performance. Because they are self-powered, dynamic microphones are ready to use simply by plugging them into a preamp—that is, the "mic level" input of your mixer or multi-track recorder, or a separate, stand-alone unit.

The second type of microphones are *condenser* mics. These work on an electrostatic principle to convert sound into current. It only takes a minimal amount of sound to move the charged particles inside a condenser microphone; as a result, these mics are very sensitive, and pick up subtleties, nuances, and tone exceptionally well. Some cannot handle heavy sound pressure levels (SPL); others can handle moderate to heavy SPL. (When I say "heavy SPL," I mean loud guitar amps and certain drums; in the case of vocals, you'll rarely find a vocalist who is "too loud" for the mic.) Condenser microphones do an amazing job at recording every little nuance in a vocal. Plus, they can have variable polar patterns for picking up sound from different directions or multiple sources.

Condensers are usually powered by an external source called *phantom power* (48 volts). This means that, unless your condenser mic uses an internal battery, it will draw power from whatever you plug it into—mixer, or external preamp. Though phantom power has become a standard feature on most such units, you should check to be sure yours has it before you purchase a brand-new condenser mic (otherwise, when you plug it in, it just won't work). Condensers, by the way, can be solid-state, tube (a.k.a. "valve"), or a hybrid of both; these terms refer to how the mic processes the input signal, which to a greater or lesser degree will affect its sound (much like with a guitar amp).

For studio and home recording, I strongly recommend a condenser microphone over a dynamic. In the past, condenser mics were not always affordable to the average consumer. Today, things are much different. Although I believe that you get what you pay for—you can spend as much as $10,000 or as little as $100 for a good microphone, and the differences in cost will be audible—condenser microphones have, by and large, become more affordable to the everyday home engineer.

Let Your Ears Decide

What are the factors involved in choosing a microphone? Well, everyone is entitled to their own opinion, so let your ears decide. You should looking for a microphone that is best suited for the vocalist. Are the vocals breathy, scratchy, clear, loud, soft? Most pro studios have a wide variety of microphones to choose from. I'm going to assume that you don't. Before you get overwhelmed in trying to choose microphones, remember that a mic is just a means to an end. Your goal is to capture a great vocal performance.

I'm going to give a few examples recorded with different microphones, just to see if you can hear the differences between them. Listen to TRACKS 1-3. What do you notice about the three different qualities? Ignore the vocal performance, and listen to the sound and texture of each take.

TRACK 1: _____

TRACK 2: _____

TRACK 3: _____

Let me help you, in case you're having trouble. After listening to all three tracks, did you notice how TRACK 2 sounded full, but the least clear of all three? Or did you notice how TRACK 1 sounded clear but thinner compared to TRACK 3? Did you notice how TRACK 3 was the fullest of all three performances?

The levels were all set the same; the microphones just had different responses to the voice and translated it differently. Which were condenser microphones? Which ones were dynamic? Can you tell? Which one would you choose to use after listening to them? (The answers to the different microphones used are in the back of the book. But listen first, before you go and ruin the experiment by using your eyes instead of your ears.)

Polar Patterns

What do you need your microphone to do? In other words, are you recording more than one vocalist at a time? Are you in an acoustically tuned room, or in your bedroom? What I'm trying to determine is whether or not you need a selectable polar pattern. A *polar pattern* determines how, or in what directions, the microphone picks up sound (it has nothing to do with recording in extremely cold weather!). Condenser microphones can come with different polar patterns, and each pattern has its own advantages depending on your particular recording situation.

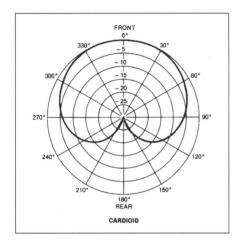

Cardioid

The most common pattern for condenser mics is cardioid. Cardioid patterns respond to sound mainly from the front of the mic, less from the sides, and reject sound from the rear. This is good for recording one voice at a time. It's also good for capturing "close mic" vocals for an intimate sound. Cardioid is generally the best choice for rejecting unwanted room sound—something to remember if your room hasn't been tuned or soundproofed.

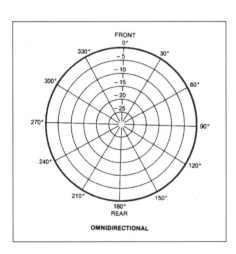

Omni-Directional

Omni, which means *all*, receives sound in a 360-degree circle. This is good for recording choir vocals, multiple-voice backing vocals, or any vocal situation with three or more people singing at the same time. It also picks up a lot of room sound on solo vocals, if you happen to like the sound of the room in which you're recording.

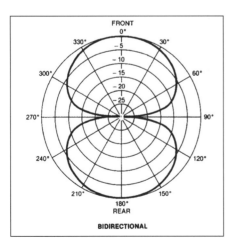

Bi-Directional

Commonly known as *figure 8*, a bi-directional pattern picks up sounds on the front and back of the mic, while rejecting sound from the sides. This works well for duets or backing vocals with two singers recording at the same time. I usually prefer using two separate mics in these situations, or recording them one after the other; some performers, however, respond best to singing in the same room at the same time. If you don't have two microphones, this could be the best option available.

Okay, after reading those explanations, you might want one, two, or all three polar patterns. If you think you'll be happy with cardioid, almost all microphones have this pattern as a default setting. (If a mic has just one setting, it will probably be cardioid. Cardioid is also the most common pattern for dynamic mics.) Incidentally, there are other polar patterns out there—e.g., hyper-cardioid and super-cardioid—but those are for more specific instrumental applications. For recording vocals, the above patterns are all that you'll need.

If you can afford a mic with switchable polar patterns, locate the front of the mic and choose one of the appropriate settings. The settings are labeled using the polar pattern pictures.

Pad

Many condenser microphones have a built-in attenuation switch, commonly known as a *pad*. This reduces the amount of input signal so the microphone doesn't distort when recording loud sounds. I've recorded several singers who simply belted out the vocals and were too loud for the microphone. When this happens, I can either back the singer farther away from the mic, or turn on the pad (if there is one). Backing the singer away tends to dilute the performance and bring in more room sound. Adding a 10 or 20 dB (decibel) pad instead allows me to keep the vocalist at the same distance and just reduce the overloading signal. You may find it beneficial to have this option in your microphone.

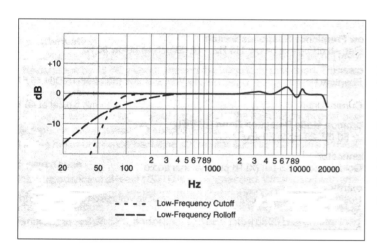

Roll-Off

A *roll-off* is a filter built in to the microphone. It generally removes sounds beneath a chosen frequency. The picture at left shows both a roll-off and a cut-off. The cut-off is removing frequencies lower than 80Hz at a rate of 18dB/octave, while the roll-off is gradually removing frequencies starting just above 200Hz at a rate of 6dB/octave.

Roll-off and/or cut-off are used to reduce ultra-low and overall low-end frequencies caused by proximity effect and movement. *Proximity effect* happens when a source is too close to the microphone. It exaggerates the amount of low end present in the sound. A little might be fine, but too much can muddy your sound. Movement of the mic or the mic stand can also generate low frequency noise, which some people refer to as "rumble." Listen to TRACK 4. This unnecessary noise, or "rumble," could have been reduced with a roll-off, which was used in TRACK 5. Remember that it's also filtering out these frequencies in your vocals, so be careful with how high the setting goes. A simple test is to sing and record some vocals and listen for the difference not in the noise, but in the lower part of the vocals. If you can't hear any difference with the roll-off in or out, as far as the vocals go, you should be safe.

Just remember that you are listening to ultra-low frequencies, and the monitors you're listening with should be able to play them back whenever present. In other words, listening for low end on a small woofer is not an accurate test environment. Using a large woofer (15" +) or a subwoofer system would be desirable. If you couldn't hear the difference in the last audio example, then your system is not accurate enough for roll-off decisions.

Other Factors

Of course, budget can be a crucial factor in what type of microphone you record with. How much can you spend on a vocal mic? (Again, costs vary between $100 and $10,000.) You may already have a microphone and wish to use that one. In my personal experience, when I'm in the studio, I use what's available to me, and it's usually a nice, high-end condenser mic. When shopping for microphones for my own home studio, I rented a variety of condensers that I could afford (as well as some I couldn't!) and just ran them through different vocal tests before making my selection. These are some things I was looking for:

1.) **Low Self-noise.** I don't want a microphone with a lot of self-noise. Because I like using moderate to heavy amounts of compression, the mic needed to be as silent as possible.

2.) **Transparency.** I'm not looking for a microphone that colors the sound too much. My goal was to find the mic that had the flattest frequency response. All microphones have a booklet with a diagram, showing how the mic responds to the frequency spectrum. (See below.) Most have a boost in the mid- to high-frequency range. This helps the sound retain clarity and adds a bit of brightness. A lot of frequencies can get lost when running through wires and cables and connectors. The example below shows a boost between 5kHz and 16kHz.

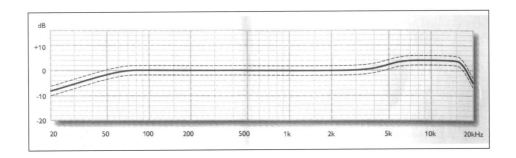

3.) **Sensitivity.** I would like a microphone that picks up the subtle nuances of any vocal. I've found that condensers react better than dynamic mics in this respect. Again, I'm not recording a live sound gig, where feedback would be a big concern. I can control my environment (unlike in a club setting), so dynamic mics are simply not my first choice.

4.) **Versatility.** Because I'm not rich, I was looking for a mic that was able to do more than record just one type of vocals. Some mics sound amazing on one person and average on others. This is great when you can afford to buy several microphones, or you believe that there will only be one need for your mic. Having said this, I also chose the mic that was most pleasing to my own vocal style, which is breathy and very close and personal. In order to test it with other sounds, I called some of my vocal friends, female and male. I listened to how the mic responded to their particular vocal characteristics and made sure that I was still pleased with the microphone's results.

For my own decision, I went with a Neumann TLM103. It filled all of my needs, and it fit my budget. A solid-state condenser mic, it's very sensitive yet can handle most vocals without distorting. The polar pattern is fixed cardioid, and there's no roll-off or pad. I find it has a pleasant character, without adding or taking away from the original vocal. This was the microphone I used to record TRACK 3, and it's also the mic used for all subsequent CD tracks.

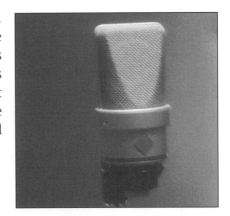

Mic Placement

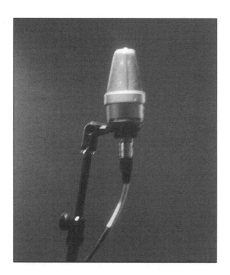

Okay, let's get started. Take your microphone and attach it to a stand. I'm going to do these examples with the microphone in a fixed position. This should help us control the distance of the singer from the mic. It will also reduce low-end rumble and other noises that can appear when you hold the mic.

Finding the Sweet Spot

A microphone has something known as a "sweet spot." (I first learned this term in baseball; a baseball bat also has a sweet spot. Help at all? Maybe not.) A sweet spot with a microphone is the place where it picks up sound best. The way to find it is by test searching. Hold out an open vocal sound like "hey" or "aah." Be sure to be no more than 3 inches away from the front of the diaphragm.

If you are the singer and engineer, you're going to need a pair of headphones to monitor yourself. While singing the open vowel sound, move from side to side, and up and down, slowly. Somewhere, directly in front of the mic is a point at which the sound is loudest and fullest. It would seem easy to locate the direct center by sight, but use your ears. Where and how the sound comes out of your mouth, and the angle at which your head is when you sing, can change everything. Half an inch can make a big difference. Take a listen to TRACK 6, and see if you can hear the sweet spot. All I did was move from left to right, passing by the sweet spot. You should be able to clearly hear the vocal sound reach its fullest at about the middle of the example. We are going to use this sweet spot as our center position for the vocals.

Which Side Is the Front?

Which side of your microphone is the front? If there is a polar pattern symbol, then that side is the front. If there is only one manufacturer's logo, then that side is the front. If you look at how the mic connects to the XLR cable (mic cable), the three pins will be in a triangle. The triangle tip points to the back, so the other side is the front.

polar pattern

manufacturer's logo

XLR connection

If your microphone is round, it can still have a "front," which is better known as "on-axis." Everything around the microphone is off-axis. If you have a shotgun-style microphone that's slender in size, it is pointing to the front, so the top is technically the "front."

round and shotgun (dynamic)

shotgun (condenser)

FYI: I usually don't recommend shotgun-style condenser mics for vocals, as they're better suited for recording acoustic guitars, hi-hats, cymbals, etc.

Distance from the Mic

How far away from the mic should the vocalist be? That really depends on the type of vocals you're recording. For breathy, soft, or intimate vocals, I recommend *close miking* technique. This would be 1 to 3 inches away with a pop screen in between. For moderate volume and loud, belting powerhouses, the mic needs to be farther away. You can back it off as far as you need to in order to keep the sound from overloading (distorting) the microphone—anywhere from 4 in. to 1 ft. would be my recommendation.

This is taking into consideration a couple of things. One, that you are going to use compression while recording. If you don't, the singer is going to have to use mic technique (moving back and forth from the microphone) in order to keep from overloading your multitrack recorder. Two, that your microphone can handle the volumes at these relatively close distances without distorting. If the mic can't handle the input signal from the vocalist, then the singer is going to have to increase the distance between him/herself and the mic; I've recorded some singers as far as 3 feet away, but this is really not an optimal solution, as the voice tends to sound thinner at such distances, room reflection sounds increase, etc. This is where a pad comes in handy. If your mic has one, then it's not necessary to move away; just switch the pad on. This should stop the overload problem.

But here is my other recommendation: Instead of moving the mic farther away, simply raise and angle it to the bridge of the singer's nose (see below right). I've found that most singers resonate in this so-called "mask" area. Because I use sensitive microphones, there is almost no loss in clarity. (Actually, except for breathy examples, the sound that comes directly out of the mouth is quite harsh; there is a lot of focused air that doesn't react well with the mic.) If you use this positioning, you don't need a pop screen, and you don't have to back the mic "away" from the singer. See if you can tell that I used this position for all of the vocal examples from here on. Try it and see if it works for you.

Why are we staying so close to the mic? First of all, we need the best signal-to-noise ratio we can get for recording quality. *Noise* is any sound other than the vocals. This includes sounds near or in the room like fans, florescent lights, neighbors, plumbing, A/C, etc. Secondly, I want to isolate the vocals from the sound of the room as much as possible. The farther away the mic is, the more it picks up reflections in the room. And lastly, I've noticed that the recorded voice sounds thinner when the mic is more than 6 inches away. I don't want to lose any of the richness of the vocals, but at the same time I am trying not to exaggerate the proximity effect that happens at close range to the mouth.

Straight-On vs. Angled Placement

The most common placement for a vocal microphone is straight on. When you have a pop screen, and a vocalist who is proficient with vocal technique regarding popping consonants, this placement works well.

However, there are times when this is not the case. Like when you don't have a pop screen, or the singer is untrained and "all over the place" dynamically. When this happens, I've found using the previously mentioned angled position produces the best results. The mic is positioned at the height of the nose, with a slight downward angle.

straight-on

angled

An angled mic position picks up more of the nasal cavity resonance, which almost all singers use. Before you freak out about the word "nasal," please understand something. When someone is said to have a "nasal quality," like a person with a cold, it's the opposite of nasal. Think about it. When you have a cold, your nose is congested or blocked up. It sounds that way because of the lack of resonance from the nose (or *mask* in singers' terms). Just hold your nose and talk. This is not nasal! It is the *lack* of nasal quality.

Now that we've cleared that up, you may find this angled mic position more desirable. It allows the singer to concentrate on singing, without worrying about a pop screen or undesirable consonants. Since we haven't moved the mic farther away from the vocalist, we don't have to worry about noise problems. Remember that when you're using a condenser microphone, it will still pick up all of the sounds coming out of the singer's mouth. Most of the blasting-type sounds, however, have been reduced. By slightly angling the mic, I reduce the amount of projection slamming the diaphragm. It's the same principle used in miking up speaker cabinets: To get a more musical quality out of an amp, the mic is angled with the cone. The main output of sound brushes past the mic, instead of hitting it dead on. Think of it like letting the sound waves gradually seep into the mic instead of confronting them head on and getting pushed hard.

Whether the singer is male or female will not change my basic set-up. How they sing will change it. I've recorded male singers who are as soft as a whisper, and females who belt louder than elephants. Soft singers get close (1") mic placement. Louder singers get the angled placement if the overall sound is too harsh or unpleasant.

Avoiding (or Using) Proximity Effect

I mentioned proximity effect earlier. Whenever a sound source is closer than normal to a microphone, the low end will be exaggerated. Remember: it's not just getting louder, it's adding more low end than any other frequency. For a thin vocal, you can use this to your advantage. However, if you listen to most vocals on professional CDs, you'll notice that the vocals by themselves are not very boomy, or heavy on low end. Let's listen to TRACK 7. This vocal has too much proximity effect. Notice the problem with select consonants, like "w" and "b." Now listen to TRACK 8, which has the same vocal line, but recorded farther away from the mic in order to reduce the proximity effect. (For another example of proximity effect, take a listen again to TRACK 2, recorded with a dynamic mic.)

Normal distance could be considered to be the size of the instrument. Your head is probably less than 12" in length, so that same distance away would be considered "normal." The closer you get, the more proximity effect there is. I know that I recommended close miking most vocals, but I also stated that you don't want the mic positioned straight into the mouth. Proximity effect happens mainly because of the air that gets moved at the recording source—so, as long as this air stream is not hitting the mic "dead on," you shouldn't have a proximity problem.

If you really must use the mic on-axis and up close, remember that too much low end makes the sound muddy, so you can't just add in as much as you want without paying the price. The ways to get around proximity effect, are first, use the roll-off on the mic. If you don't have one, I hope your mixing board has a filter. It functions the same way. Your other option is to aim the microphone more towards the mask (nose area).

Using reference CDs has been a huge help to me. Find a singer whose voice you like the sonic qualities of, and that sounds something like yours. You can use this as a basic guide to see how far you can push or take away the low-end frequencies before the sound becomes undesirable.

Using a Pop Screen

I've mentioned the pop screen before. This handy device removes excessive airflow from the mic diaphragm. Air can overload a mic easily. It usually is attached to the consonants p, b, and t. These sounds are quick and concentrated. The pop screen helps diffuse and/or deflect the sounds before they reach the microphone. If you're using close mic positioning, the use of a pop screen does not alter the distance. You just put the pop screen between the mic and the singer's lips. Try to keep the screen from touching the mic, though; otherwise, it will create a scratching sound that could be annoying. Use a gooseneck attachment or a second stand to insure that this doesn't happen.

Condenser mics react quickly to sounds, whereas dynamic mics react much slower. Dynamic microphones usually have a metal grill covering the diaphragm, thus diffusing most of the transient (fast) sounds. I'm assuming you've chosen the condenser mic for your vocals, so you might invest in a pop screen. If you're using a dynamic mic, you may not need one, or you might like the transient or punchy sounds in your music.

If you can't purchase a pop screen, I've seen people make them out of pantyhose and a hanger. If this doesn't work, use the angled, "mask" mic position, and you shouldn't have any troubles.

Positions for Backing Vocals and Duets

So far, I've been explaining single-vocalist microphone applications. What happens with backing vocals and duets? When you only have one microphone, positioning and polar patterns are everything.

Backing Vocals

Backing vocals can be viewed in two basic categories for me: tight and loose. Tight backing vocals are close miked and done individually. They are treated with as much respect as the main vocal. They are usually multitracked and layered for thickness. Many times, the lead vocalist records all of these parts him or herself. Modern R&B is a great example of tight back vocals. If this is the backing vocal sound you're going for, I recommend as little distance from the mic as possible, and giving each person their own mic.

Loose back vocals, on the other hand, have more distance to the mic (6" to 10 feet depending on the vocal blend). They have a more live feel and are sometimes done by the other band members (who aren't always the greatest singers). Everyone sings together, and each person has a distance from the mic depending on the blending of all the levels. Any form of rock or rap music is usually a good example.

Singers around front of mic (cardioid)

With one mic and a cardioid pattern, I recommend the set-up shown at left. You need to adjust the distance of the singers according to the vocal blend of their voices in the music. Remember that they can't be separated in the mix, because they are sharing a single track.

Singers in omni

If you have an omni-directional mic, you can arrange them as shown here. Again, adjust their distances based on the levels of each voice working together.

If you have two microphones, just treat each like a lead vocal, and use the straight-on or the angled/mask placement. For loose back vocals, start 6" away from each mic. For tight backing vocals, start at 1" away.

Duets

For duet vocalists who want to sing at the same time, and like being close together, I recommend using a bi-directional polar pattern. Again their distances are based on quality and blend.

Not all microphones have a bi-directional polar pattern, so as an alternative you could use omni. I would still position the singers in a "figure 8" as shown. We're going to get more reflections and unwanted room sound with an omni pattern, but we would have to make do with what we have.

Duet "figure 8" position (bi-directional or omni)

As a last resort, I would use a cardioid pattern and position the singers roughly side by side. The problem is that neither singer is "on axis" nor in the "sweet spot," so we compromise both voices in order to work as a team.

Duet "side-by-side" position (cardioid)

Compression

Compression is an important part of recording vocals. When recording any sound, your objective is to get the most sound to tape possible, without peaking. Because vocals have a very wide dynamic range, it's difficult to get the maximum levels possible, consistently.

Think about it: vocals are one of the most expressive instruments around; not only are there countless nuances to every performance but also constantly changing volumes. If it were only a solo vocal performance, this would not cause too many engineering difficulties. But usually a vocal is part of a song, with other sounds—like drums, bass, guitar, etc. These other instruments don't have as wide of a dynamic range. Do you see where I'm headed? If the drums are staying consistent in level, and the singer gets quieter, what happens to the mix? You guessed it; the vocals get drowned out. Not good! And what if the vocals are pushing hard, but the other instruments are consistent? Right again. The vocals jump out and sound uncomfortable.

Listen to TRACK 9. I've recorded a vocal without compression; it's the same line that you heard on TRACKS 1-3, but this time with music. In order to teach you about compression, I've left the vocal track completely dry (without effects). Did you notice how the words are getting lost in the mix? If I raised the volume in order to bring up the low levels, then it would distort on the louder phrases. Notice how the level swells up and down, and is uncomfortable to listen to. I'd like to use compression to control the overall dynamics so that the vocal sits better in the song. Now listen to TRACK 10. This track is compressed to bring up the softer parts that were getting lost before. The levels are more consistent and up front. Are you interested in how it's done? Just read on…

One Simple Goal

In live sound applications, a singer will usually vary the distance of the mic from their mouth in order to keep a consistent output level. So when they're loud, they'll back off the mic, and when they're soft they'll get closer to it. This keeps everything as even as possible.

In the studio, however, we're going to use compression. Why? First, levels being recorded to tape are much more sensitive than live sound coming through speakers. If the recorded level gets too loud, it will distort, and not in a good way. Second, I'm going to assume that most of you are using a digital recording medium (hard disc, mini disc, digital tape, etc.) and not an analog medium. Analog tape naturally compresses the sound when you begin to hit above the peak. Digital, unfortunately, does not. It just clips and distorts. Third, when you record in the studio, it is important to keep the vocal level consistent without changing its color or tone. When you move the mic around, you change the amount of room sound involved, and also the overall vocal sound. Very annoying and unprofessional! So, by using a compressor, we are going to keep the vocal signal from peaking, and also give a little more body to our softer, breathier parts. Sound good?

The most difficult part about getting the right compressor settings is understanding this one simple goal: *We are trying to make the compression unnoticeable.* Later in the chapter, I'll go over some more radical settings, but the basic concept is about keeping it discrete. Because of the misunderstanding of the function of compression, most people use too much, because that's when you can really hear it. By then, it is too excessive for most people's tastes, and they get frustrated, or think that compression is an evil device (which is not true!).

Control Settings & Terminology

Okay, with that out of the way, let's look at the settings on a compressor. With all the different types of compressors available, there are many different names for the same settings. I'll start with the most common terms.

Threshold

Threshold is the level above which compression begins. When the sound goes above this level, the compressor will look to the other settings to decide how much to reduce the signal. Think of the threshold as an imaginary horizontal volume border. Any part of the sound going above that line can be compressed. The sounds that stay below that line don't qualify for compression.

Ratio

Ratio is a comparison value—for example 3:1, 5:1, 2:1, etc. The first number represents the amount of decibels going into the compressor above the threshold. The second number represents the amount of decibels passing through the unit unaffected. Let's take 3:1, for example. For every 3 decibels above the threshold setting, only 1 passes through to the output. What happens to the other 2? They get compressed. So if at any point the vocals are 9 decibels louder than the threshold setting, only 3 decibels will pass through to the output, and the other 6 get compressed. By allowing some decibels to pass through, you will get a natural increase in dynamics, even though the compressor is stopping the majority of the peak sound. Thus, the higher the ratio setting, the smaller the dynamic range. But remember, if you set your threshold so high that none of the sound peaks above it, the highest ratio in the world won't do anything. Only the part of the sound above the threshold gets a ratio applied to it.

Attack

Attack is a measurement of the time it takes for the compression ratio to be applied. Even though the sound has gone above the threshold, there is still an adjustable time (usually in milliseconds) that the compressor "waits" before applying compression. This allows the sound to "breathe" or sound more natural. Some of the peaks will still get through to tape. With vocals, unlike some other instruments, this may not be desirable. The sounds that usually get through are popping noises and harsh consonants. We're going to use the attack time to limit the passing of these sounds. When the attack is slower, the sound becomes punchier because the peak of the sound slips through before the ratio is applied.

Release

Release is also a time measurement. It decides how long the ratio is applied, after the sound volume has dropped below the threshold. If the compressor just turned off instantly when the sound dropped below the threshold, we would noticeably hear the change. Also, the sound might quickly hover around the threshold, going above and below, and we would again hear the change in the compressor turning on and off. This is sometimes referred to as "pumping" and "breathing." We would like a more natural change in the way the compressor reacts to the drop in sound volume. Shorter release times allow for more sustain, while longer settings tighten up the sound's decay.

Make-Up/Gain/Output

Whichever name your compressor has for this feature, the purpose is the same. For every decibel you lose to compression, you adjust this knob to compensate equally. Say you're using 8 decibels of compression (shown on your dB reduction meter). You then adjust the output to +8dB. With every decibel of reduction you use, the peaks become less erratic and more consistent. This allows you to increase the amount of level going to your recorder, without fear of overloading. Get the idea? More sound to tape with less fear of distortion. What a wonderful concept! Some people use this knob more aggressively than the 1 dB lost = 1 dB gain, and then it becomes an extension of your fader level to tape. Depending on the quality and quietness of your compressor, you might enjoy using this gain stage a little more than usual.

Some compressors have automatic gain stages. This means that you have no control over the amount of output. The compressor will adjust the output according to the amount of compression you are using.

dB Reduction Meter

Somewhere on the front of your compressor is a meter (VU, LED, LCD) that shows you the amount of compression being applied. Sometimes you have a dual/triple function meter and need to switch to see the different readouts, usually input/output/gain reduction. It will either measure in the positive or in the negative, but it makes no difference. 3dB of reduction is 3 decibels regardless of whether the readout is +3 or -3. When someone says that they used about 5dB of compression on a sound, this is the meter that gave them that reading. It is very common to express compression in these terms, and this meter is your final answer to the equation you created by adjusting the threshold, ratio, release, and attack knobs.

If your compressor lacks any of these settings, then it's likely that they are fixed settings. You can find out what the settings are by looking at the manual. Many compressors lack variable attack and release times. They are predetermined, and you need to refer to your manual to figure out what they are set at. Other compressors give different names for the same settings. Since this book isn't about compressors, I'll leave it to you to figure out which features are the ones listed above.

The Signal Path: Recording vs. Mixing

Where do you put the compressor in the signal path? Well, if you have a separate compressor device, you would want to follow a signal path similar to one of these in order to maximize your compressor results:

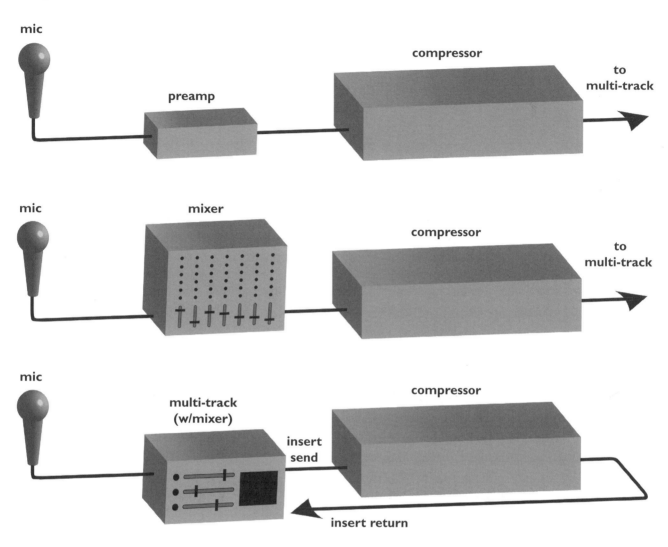

NOTE: If you're recording to hard disk and using internal software for compression, then the above connections will be internal.

One word of caution about doing it this way. You are recording your compressor results, and they cannot be changed later. It is very important to remember that once you can actually "hear" the compression, you've gone too far for most people's tastes. If you like excessive compression (and it is a great sound sometimes), I recommend you save that type of compression for when you mix. The signal flow for that would look like this:

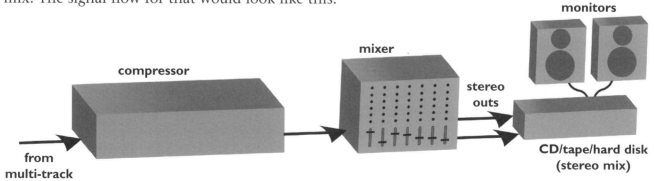

It is possible, and commonly advised, that you use some compression while you record and some while you mix. In a professional situation, this allows you flexibility at both stages. During recording, I'm compressing to get the most out of my vocal, without altering the desirable qualities inherent to the voice. When I mix, I'm more concerned with having the vocal "fit" into the mix among the other instruments. Compression during mixing helps me control the vocal level and dynamics in relation to the other sounds in the mix. Many engineers choose to "ride the fader" (or use an automated fader control) instead of applying compression in order to do this. I've used one or the other and sometimes both. It really depends on whether you're using professional quality compressors or not.

Please remember: if you're using a computer software plug-in for compression, check to see if the plug-in occurs before or after the sounds are recorded to hard disk. You can do this simply by recording with the plug-in turned on, and then, during playback, turning it off. If the vocal reverts back to the uncompressed sound, then the plug-in is active only after recording.

You may or may not be able to hear the difference between compression applied before recording versus after recording. For me, it's a big difference. Remember that compression, while reducing certain frequencies, increases others. It does not "create" frequencies; it can only magnify ones that already exist. If you compress after recording, any frequencies that were lost during recording won't "magnify" well afterward. Imagine enlarging a picture that is already "grainy." What happens? It gets even grainier! But what if the picture had less "graininess" when it was taken? What if the "focus" was better from the beginning? Then it "magnifies" better later. This is how I view sound. If you record it weak, then it can only be a "big weak" sound later on with compression. However, if you record with compression, the sound may be small, but it won't be weak, and later on it can truly be made bigger.

Getting Started: Using Compression on a Full Voice

When recording any instrument, your first step is always to set levels. With or without compression, your goal is to get the most sound to tape—without overloading and causing distortion—and this can take a little trial and error. Connect your mic to a preamp, send that level to a recorder, and then have your vocalist run through their part a few times. You're going to set the level to the recorder while the vocalist is singing. Ask the singer to sing the "loudest" line in the song (make sure the singer is warmed up first), so you can find the "peak level." This vocal sound should be set just below clipping on your recorder. How do you know where the clipping point is? Some recorders have a red meter that indicates clipping; others, you'll have to do by ear. In order to do it by ear, you increase the level to tape while monitoring the sound that's coming out of your recorder, and when you hear clipping or distortion, you reduce the level until the clipping goes away. I've found that sometimes the meters are not calibrated properly, so always use your ears over your eyes. And in order to find the actual "peak" point on the various recorders I've used, I always make the sound peak just a little, in order to be able to back it off to the appropriate non-peaking level. Just remember that vocals will vary depending upon the emotional need to hit certain notes, and the comfort level of the singer. Some singers only start opening up after a good half hour (or a couple shots of whiskey!). Other singers will get softer as the session wears on because they get tired easily. Setting levels is a process that may happen more than once in the session.

Once your basic levels have been set, and you're set to record distortion-free, then you're ready to add compression. So that we can focus exclusively on compression here, we'll use a pre-recorded vocal as an example. To get started, record TRACK 11 onto your recording device, or have an uncompressed vocal ready to use.

Step 1: Observe Your Levels

I know I just discussed this, but it's the first step in applying compression at both recording and mixing stages: Notice the level changes in the vocal—not just with your ears, but also with your eyes on the meter. What you hear and what the computer "hears" are two different things. What seems like a consistent level to you can have an unstable level on your recording meters. Consonants that produce a lot of air (like p's) are much "louder" for the tape machine than for you. This is because when you listen, you stand a healthy three feet away from someone's mouth (more if they have bad breath). The microphone, however, is much closer and has to react to sounds much sooner than our ears would. This is why proximity effect and popping sounds can be a problem. I've used my angled mic technique to reduce this problem

Step 2: Set the Threshold

Now that you've looked at our vocal take, let's start to compress it. So where do you set the threshold? Look at your output meter for the vocal take you are using. I want you to find the loudest peak on the meter. Then I want you to listen for the softest vocal word and find the meter reading at that point.

In TRACK 11, the loudest peak is at 0dB on my meters with the word "hide." The softest word is "look" at –20dB. This is the range to set my threshold, between 0 and –20. If I set the threshold high, closer to 0, there is less chance for compression and less of the sound to compress. This would be ideal for light, or soft, compression. If I were looking for a lot of compression, I would set the threshold low, closer to –20dB, but not below that; I wouldn't want to compress, or limit, the sounds that are already too low in the track (that would defeat my goal of trying to get the most recorded sound to tape). Keep in mind that this 0 dB to –20 dB range is describing the "attacks" of the sound, not the decay. Decay or endings of sounds are even softer than –20 dB.

I usually just start with the threshold halfway between the highest and lowest vocal levels. After trying different places, I used –14dB as my threshold for TRACK 10.

Step 3: Apply a Ratio

No matter where you choose to start with your threshold, you're going to have no compression without a ratio applied to the sound. So now we're going to choose a ratio setting. There are many different schools of thought about what ratio is the correct one for a vocal. For me, it depends on a couple of things. First, how much overall compression is going to be needed to get the job done? If the answer is "a lot" or "tons," then I'm going to need a higher ratio to get the results I need (6:1 and up). If the answer is anything from moderate to minimal, then I can get away with lower ratios (4:1 and lower).

The other factor that I always keep in mind is how good the compressor sounds. Most compressors are not completely discrete. In some instances, they're very colorful. If the compressor sounds good (like a nice tube compressor, an 1176, etc.), then I don't mind having the compressor altering my sound. Sometimes, I prefer it. By using low ratios (3:1 and down), I can set the threshold very low, and process most of the sound through the compressor. The lower the ratio, the lower my threshold setting can be, and the more the compressor is "on" when the vocal is happening. On the other side, let's take a not-so-subtle compressor (or "cheap piece of junk" brand). I don't want the compressor working unless it has to. In other words, I will have the threshold as high as possible, leaving most of the vocal untouched. In order to still obtain my desired result—printing the most sound to tape—I'll need to apply a higher ratio (6:1 and up), so that when the threshold is met and the compressor is "on," it's really limiting those peaks and thereby keeping the levels consistent overall.

Sound confusing? Let's just work on the vocal in TRACK 11. With the ratio at 1:1, I will have no compression. I adjust to 2:1, and the compressor starts to work. For me though, 2:1 is not leveling out the sound enough. How do I know? I've placed the vocal with the music and still lost some words. Eventually, I found 6:1 to be a decent place (TRACK 10). When the ratio was higher (10:1 and up), it squashed my loud sounds. Oh, did I forget to mention? Nothing in life is free. The compressor has to reduce the louder sounds in order to make room for the softer ones. This means it affects the louder sounds the most, and not always in a positive way. Once I notice the compressor squeezing the louder words, I back off the ratio or raise the threshold. This is a good way to gauge how much compression you're using, by listening and making sure that you can't hear the squeeze on the louder sounds. Need an example of squeezing? Listen to TRACK 12. The vocals are definitely more even, but the compressor is suffocating the louder phrases. You can hear the compressor react to the words "try" and "someone" and "hide." It's no longer discrete, so I'm going to back off.

Again, I can go back and adjust my threshold and then re-adjust the ratio. The goal is to get the levels in a dynamic range that stays with the music. The guide marker is in trying to keep the compressor unnoticeable.

Step 4: Adjust Gain/Make-Up

Right now, it probably doesn't sound any better (unless you have an automatic gain make-up stage). This is because all we've really done is reduce the vocal. It's time to make up for the levels we've taken away. Since I reduced the levels by 7dB (as shown on my dB reduction meter), I adjusted the output 7dB higher, without fear of distorting. Check your dB reduction meter. What does it read at its highest point? You can adjust your output to that setting. Now how does it sound? It should sound fuller and bigger, and be perceived as louder, although the peak level is still the same as before. It's just that now that everything beneath our peak level has been brought up closer to the loudest sound.

Step 5: Set Attack & Release

Now for some finishing touches on the "unnoticeable" part. First of all, if you can "hear" the compressor turning on, then it's possible that your attack setting is too fast. When the attack is too fast, the sound "ducks" or "pumps" instead of gradually reducing the peak. Listen again to TRACK 12 as an example. For TRACK 10, I had the attack setting at 7ms in order to smooth out all of the vocal attacks. If the attack setting is too long, the peaks will not be brought down in time, and the sound will not be able to brought under control.

Most importantly in the final touches is the release. I only want the compressor to stay on as long as the sound is peaking. The release setting decides how long the compressor stays on after the sound has dropped below the threshold. So you're thinking that the release should be 0, right? Wrong. Remember that I want the compressor to be unnoticeable. If it's constantly turning on and off, it's not going to be to discrete, now is it? So I'm going to need to use the release to create a "natural" turning off of the compressor. If it's too short, it sounds like TRACK 13. Notice how you can hear the compressor turning off and back on. But if the release is too long, the compressor keeps compressing the sound, even though the levels are below the threshold. This "squashes" the sound. Remember TRACK 12? In TRACK 10, I used around 50ms for the release.

Listen now to TRACK 14. This is the vocal by itself, but compressed. Compare this example with the original uncompressed vocal on TRACK 11, so you can hear how much fuller and consistent the sound is.

For Falsetto/Softer Sounds

Sometimes compression is used to help a smaller voice get bigger. Now, I wouldn't be using the compressor based on dynamics; I would be using it to control the soft sound, and then print levels as high as possible to the recorder. Because soft voices usually don't have big dynamic ranges, the "squeezing" sound normally associated with lots of compression is not a factor. The compressor will be on consistently and it will be hard to notice, because the tone won't change.

Listen to TRACK 15. It's a small, soft vocal part. Listen to TRACK 16. This is what happens when it gets put in a mix. It sounds even smaller against all the other tracks. Now listen to TRACK 17. This is the vocal part compressed. Notice how much fuller and bigger it sounds.

Let me address a big misconception right now. How many of you think that TRACK 17 just sounds louder? Be honest. Let me explain why you are misguided. When recording to a digital multitrack, you can only record levels as high as "0" on the meter. What happens when you go higher and peak in the red? You clip or distort. So you can only record as high as your loudest vocal part. Most of the time, the vocal sits in its normal level. Every now and then it drops below this standard level, and also goes above that level about as often. You have to set your levels based on the few loud peaks, however, not your consistent vocal level. This means you still have printed levels at "0," just not that consistently.

On the other hand, compression allows the vocal to stay at the peak level more often, and thus sounds "louder." It's not any louder at the peaks; it is consistently closer to peaking, and thus it sounds fuller and bigger overall. Again, it still has the same peak point as an uncompressed signal, it just gets to stay closer to that point more often than uncompressed signals. Make sense? If not, you can always e-mail me...

Let's get back to the example. Compare TRACK 15 and TRACK 17. Big difference, huh? Now listen to TRACK 18, and notice how much easier the vocal sits in the mix. Compare TRACK 16 and TRACK 18 to get the big picture.

The reason I keep trying to explain this over and over is because recording in the studio is a whole different animal than singing live. You don't have to sing over the band anymore. The studio is a controlled environment that should allow the singer to focus on expression and tone, and not on belting to be heard over the other instruments in the song. It's your job as an engineer to capture the performance and make it work in the mix.

Using a Sidechain

Maybe your compressor has the ability to sidechain. This means that if you put two signals into the compressor, one will trigger the settings on the compressor, while the other will be the sound being affected. Sound a little confusing? Well, basically you need to "mult" or split your one vocal sound and get a copy of the first in any way that you can (patchbay, insert send, Y cable, etc.). One of these sounds goes to an EQ first, before it goes into the sidechain input of your compressor. The other signal goes directly into the compressor's normal input. Now, the sidechain input is the one the compressor listens to in order to decide how much compression to apply. But it's the normal input signal that actually gets the compression applied to it.

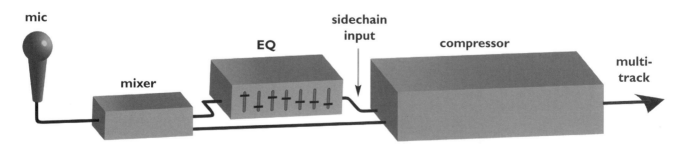

With this ability, you can set the compressor to be frequency responsive, instead of just responsive to overall levels. How about an audio example? Listen to TRACK 19. This is a vocal line that has been compressed heavily. At its maximum, it reached 13dB of gain reduction from a ratio of 10:1. You know what? You can hear the compression working on just about every line. You can hear the squeezing. Now listen to TRACK 20. This is the same vocal. It has the same ratio and the same amount of compression at its maximum. But this one has sidechain input connected. The EQ that I used removed 215Hz and 550Hz with wide bell settings. It also added a few decibels of 3.5kHz. What this means is that the compressor was less sensitive to the low frequencies mentioned, and therefore reacted less in regards to compressing when it heard these frequencies. It also compressed more when the 3.5kHz frequency range was being produced by the vocal. (NOTE: If you don't understand the Hz and kHz terminology, read the next chapter on EQ.)

So what did the vocal sound like in comparison to the vocal without the sidechain? Well, right from the first line, it was smoother and more discrete. It didn't compress the lines that were lower, and therefore they became bigger because of it. The only squeezing that happened was on the beginning of the lines "try to find" and "hide inside." And even then, it was brief and only on the initial word, not the whole line. Sidechaining helps smooth out the compressor. This can allow you to use a lot of compression but still maintain the discrete quality we're looking for.

Creating a De-esser

Compression can also be triggered by an equalizer to create a *de-esser*. The job of the de-esser is to lessen the effects of sibilance. Sibilance is the name for the "sss" sound that pierces your ears sometimes during a vocal. The "sss" sound sits in a particular frequency range, usually between 5kHz and 10kHz. A de-esser "senses" these frequencies and compresses them when they are too loud.

The way it works is this: Using your sidechain input, make sure that the EQ setting is *boosting* the "sss" sound of the vocal. The compressor will then think that the "sss" sounds are too loud and compress every time an "sss" sound is heard. (Again, with a sidechain, the sidechain input is never heard by the listener, only by the device. The normal input is what is affected and what actually passes through the unit.) Again, it only compresses a certain frequency range. You simply increase the amount of reduction until the "sss" sound is not too loud for your tastes. You want to be careful not to use too much, or otherwise the vocal can become dull. Most professional vocalists are conscious of how much they pronounce their "sss" sounds, and usually moderate the proper amount. Most novice engineers end up boosting too much high end on a vocal track, thus creating a sibilance problem. I think that if you print maximum levels to tape and use a compressor wisely, you shouldn't have to crank up the high end on an EQ.

Equalization

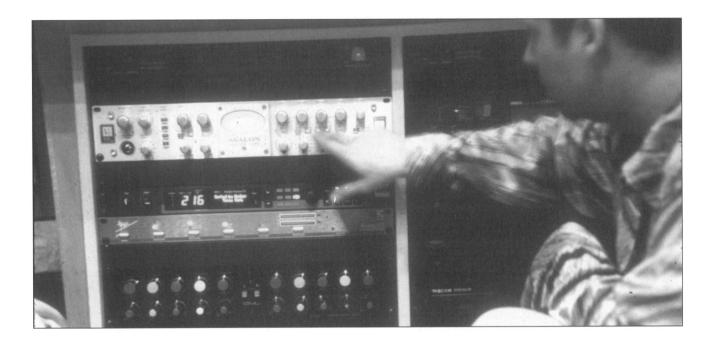

An equalizer is a device designed to change the frequencies within a sound. It can either boost or cut a selected amount of frequencies at the same time.

Graphic vs. Parametric

Equalizers are divided into two categories: graphic and parametric. A *graphic* EQ generally has sliders that move up and down in order to boost or cut particular frequencies (indicated below each slider). Therefore, the frequencies are fixed and cannot be changed. The good side is that a graphic EQ usually has many bands or frequencies to choose from. If you are using a graphic EQ, simply boost or cut the frequencies we'll be dealing with, or the closest frequency that you have available.

A *parametric* EQ generally has knobs so you can choose from the different frequencies allowed. If they have three frequency-choice knobs, they're described as high, mid, and low frequencies. If you are not able to choose different frequency numbers (Hertz) for each band, then it's known as semi-parametric. For example, some mixers have the high fixed at 12kHz and the low at 80Hz, but the midrange can be adjusted (known as "sweepable") between 800Hz and 5kHz. A four-band parametric EQ gives you one more simultaneous frequency choice. These are divided into high frequency, high mid frequency, low mid frequency, and low frequency ranges. To also help you fine tune a bit more, they usually have a Q or bandwidth control that decides how many frequencies are affected in that area. For the EQ examples in the book, try to use the frequency mentioned or the closest available number. If a Q setting is not mentioned, leave it in the middle or around the value "2" if it doesn't have a clearly labeled halfway point.

A Practical Approach

My favorite way to understand EQ is to put it in practical terms. You can generalize how EQ makes a sound brighter, duller, fuller, nasal, or smoother, but I think that it depends a lot on the vocalist and the microphone components being used. You can get very technical with numbers and cycles, but the bottom line is understanding what you're using. I'd like you to listen to EQ in terms of how it affects the actual sounds the vocalist makes. We basically have different resonating chambers, diction, and tone to deal with. By adjusting different EQ settings, we will enhance wanted sounds, reduce unwanted ones, or give the impression of more or less resonance.

You need to know a little bit about Hertz and kiloHertz in order to understand EQ. For those of you who are experienced with frequency numbers, just use this as a review. Listen to TRACK 21. There are three oscillator tones printed at 10kHz, 1000Hz (or1kHz), and 100Hz. These tones represent the three basic areas of sound frequencies: low, middle, and high.

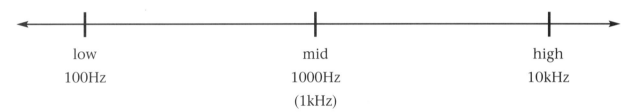

low	mid	high
100Hz	1000Hz	10kHz
	(1kHz)	

When we adjust the EQ, it will add or take away vocal overtones around these three areas. Every frequency has its own sound/pitch, so I'm just generalizing to get you started. When you listen to the following examples of how the EQ affects the vocal, it's important that you listen to the right area of the vocal sound being affected. I'll do my best to describe what I hear as we do it, so you can follow along.

Listen to TRACK 22. (You can even record it onto your multitrack and try the examples I'm going to give you on your own EQ.) This is a vocal take with no EQ or compression added. We call this "flat," meaning no processing done. What I'm going to do is change some frequencies in the four main EQ spectrums: Low, low mid-range, high mid-range, and high end. I want you to listen to the CD examples and continue to read along, in order to understand what is happening as the EQ is altered. I'll do my best to describe how it's affecting the sound, in case you don't know what to listen for.

The bottom line is that EQ is a matter of opinion when it comes to using it. Especially with vocals! This is someone's personal distinctive quality you'll be playing with. I believe that when it comes to vocals, you should use EQ as a corrective measure. This means that you should use it if you hear that something is "wrong" with the tone of the voice. What I mean by "tone" is whether it sounds thin, bright, dull, hollow, full, muddy, nasal, etc. Then, you just need to know which frequencies are responsible for adding to, or removing these types of qualities. Let's experiment with some so that you can try these during your vocal sessions.

Low (150Hz)

Listen again to TRACK 22. Let's say that you want to add more body or richness to the sound. You might feel that it sounds too thin. Listen to TRACK 23. I've added 10 decibels of 150Hz with an EQ. I've added a little more than usual, just to make it obvious as to what effect the EQ has on the sound. Because of this, you can also notice that while the vocal has more body, it also starts getting "boomy" or muddy sounding. This will help you understand why you might want to remove this frequency in a vocal track. When a singer gets too close to the mic, it can exaggerate these frequencies and cause the voice to sound "boomy."

Listen to TRACK 24. This is the same vocal, but this time I reduced 150Hz. Do you notice the change in color between TRACK 22 and TRACK 24? If you're listening on speakers that have a good bass response, you should notice that TRACK 24 sounds thin and lacking in body. But at the same time, it is clearer and more focused. Every time you add or remove EQ, there is a reaction somewhere else. It's a double-edged sword, so to speak. Pay attention every time you use EQ to what is gained and what is lost. It should be a happy trade-off.

Low Mid (800Hz)

Let's move on to 800Hz. Listen to TRACK 22 to get the original vocal in your head again. Now listen to TRACK 25. What's the difference? This might be harder to pinpoint. As far as vocal frequencies go, this is a low-midrange frequency. It still adds a certain amount of body to the vocal, but it is less muddy, less warm, and more up front than the 150Hz example. Compare TRACK 25 with TRACK 23 to hear the difference. It also accentuates the breathing sounds in the vocal. Whereas TRACK 23 added more sound from the chest of the singer, TRACK 25 is adding more of the throat.

Now listen to TRACK 22 for a moment. Then listen to TRACK 26. I've reduced 800Hz from this vocal. This lowers the throat resonance from the voice and makes it sound "scooped out" or hollow. It's mainly chest sound and mask/head sound. It makes the voice less forward sounding, but not thin like TRACK 24. This might be good to use for vocals that need to blend in more with other vocals, or other instruments in the mix.

High Mid (3kHz)

Go back to TRACK 22. I need you to do this, to ensure that your ears don't fool you. I remember being in a candle shop, smelling different scented candles, and after a while my sense of smell started to become dull. The lady behind the counter suggested that I take a break and sniff some coffee grinds. At first I thought she was a wacko. But then she explained that it would help balance my sense of smell again. This is the same thing I'm asking you to do (without the coffee). I've used the same vocal take for every example, so there are no other variables to consider.

Now listen to TRACK 27. When comparing it with TRACK 22, it sounds more forward in the speakers, more "pointy" sounding, and has more nasal or mask resonance. I've boosted 3kHz for this example, and it brings out more of the attack of the voice. If a voice wasn't cutting through the mix, I might add this frequency to bring it out more.

Listen back to TRACK 22. Now listen to TRACK 28. I've reduced 3kHz this time. The voice sounds smoother without being dull or unclear. You'll notice it especially on the word "hide" in the vocal line. In TRACK 27, it jumps out. In TRACK 28, it stays closer to the level of the other words. This can be great for helping a voice to blend when it has too much "bite."

High (10kHz)

By now, you know the drill: TRACK 22. Now listen to TRACK 29. I've added 10kHz to this vocal. The vocal becomes clearer, but depending on your monitors, it might become sibilant as well. Sibilance is that sharp "sss" sound that can get annoying when listening at loud levels. 10kHz brightens the vocal, but too much can cause spikes on "s" and "t" sounds. This is the frequency where the lips and diction are affected.

If you listen to TRACK 30, which is just the opposite of TRACK 29 (reducing 10kHz), you should feel that the vocal is dull and unclear in comparison with TRACK 22. However, it might be looked at as warmer or softer, if there wasn't so much of the frequency removed.

Ultra-High (20kHz)

Last one. Listen to TRACK 22. Okay, now listen to TRACK 31. This is adding 20kHz. Depending again on your speakers, it should sound more "open" than TRACK 22. It adds clarity, without sounding thin or shrill. The frequency is above all of the pitches of the notes, and can only accentuate the harmonics or overtones of the voice. This creates a more "open" sound that improves all of the frequencies lost, due to cables, wiring, converters, etc.

I picked specific frequencies for the vocal example that I used. I recommend that you experiment with frequencies higher or lower than the ones that I chose for your own vocal sounds. Every voice is different, and every song is different. Depending on the flexibility of your EQ, you can simultaneously add and reduce different frequencies to help shape the voice if it needs to be. The combinations are endless...

WARNING: Like compression, EQ can be applied either at the recording stage or later, during mixing. Please remember that when you "print" your EQ—that is, place it before the multitrack in your signal path when you record—you have to commit to those settings. You need to be sure, therefore, that the sound is better, because it is a permanent change. The advantage is superior quality; using EQ on a sound that was recorded poorly is simply not as effective. The trade-off, of course, is flexibility. If you wait to apply EQ until after recording, you have the ability to change up until the last moment of mixdown.

My advice? Use both approaches, but use them appropriately. When I print my EQ settings, it's to get the best possible vocal sound to tape. Many times, I'll decide that the best sound is obtainable without using any EQ at all. Later, when it's time to blend the vocal with the other tracks, I'll often use EQ to modify the sound and make it fit better with the other instruments. It's a matter of taste, musical genre, and the desired level of production you're looking for. I recommend you experiment as much as possible to find what's right for you.

Settings for "Radio" and Lo-Fi Effects

Even though I told you that EQ should be used as a corrective device, there are some cool effects that you can create with EQ. How about that "radio" or "lo-fi" sound? You know, the one that sounds like you're talking through a telephone. Here's how you achieve that effect.

Remember what we learned earlier about EQ and frequencies? Hopefully, you didn't skip it. Anyway, I'm going to remove all of the low end from 550Hz on down. I'm using a high-pass filter to do this. You make a high-pass filter by selecting a shelf for the bandwidth selection, instead of the normal bell curve. (You'll see this as a button or switch on your EQ unit, if you have it; a shelf removes all frequencies below the target, not just in the area around it, as with the normal bell curve.) If you don't have shelving options, then just try to remove as many frequencies as you can below 550Hz. This makes the vocal sound small, like it's coming out of a small speaker.

Next, I remove all the frequencies above 8kHz. This makes the vocal, which sounds small, dull and old sounding. Last but not least is a midrange boost of 1kHz. This amplifies that nasal, telephone sound. Want to hear it? Listen to TRACK 32. The first vocal line is a normal EQ setting. The second and third lines are the "radio" sounds from the EQ, and the fourth line goes back to the normal EQ.

Tracking Vocals

Creating the Right Situation

Before I get specific about tracking methods, let me help you with the overall picture first. Singing is the most personal thing in the world. Each person was born with a voice as unique as his or her fingerprints. Vocalists with lots of confidence, talent, and experience are able to make magic out of any situation. The other 95% would prefer a little outside stimulation, known as ambience.

The recording environment should be a pleasurable one. Depending on the style of music, it might be dim lights and incense or flashing lights and tons of caffeine. (I'm not even going to touch the subject of drugs, because my editor would probably erase the entire section.) The idea is to create the best atmosphere possible. This includes everything related to the five senses. Even though the engineer is mostly concerned with recording gear and the acoustics of the room, it is extremely important to keep the vibe happening. Think about these things before you record:

Who: Who is necessary at the time of recording? If someone makes the singer uncomfortable or self-conscious, they should not be around during the tracking session. (Sometimes that includes the engineer! Someone else with a little experience at running the tape machine can do the job, once the engineer gets the sounds, if necessary.)

Is there someone in the band who helps the singer with guidance of any kind? Someone outside the band? Some singers are true performers and only get in the mood when there are other people around to inspire their vocals—just don't let the session turn into a playground.

When: Schedule the session at the most convenient time, for the least amount of interruptions—especially if you have to worry about neighbors, roommates, etc. I find myself recording after midnight most of the time, just because there is no one to bother me in the studio. Mornings are almost completely out of the question for most singers. It is not the most favorable time for energy or inspiration. Don't forget to think about the singer's needs.

Schedule sessions when the singer is fresh and you have maximum focus ability. Many times, vocals are recorded after basic tracking. Well, basic tracking starts at noon and might finish by 8:00pm. 8:00pm isn't too late to start, but we've already been at it for eight straight hours. Two hours into the vocals, everyone becomes tired and careless, mistakes happen, and attention to detail is completely overlooked for sake of going home to eat and sleep. After about twelve straight hours of recording in a day, I'm a zombie. The vocals are too important to leave until the scraps of the day.

Where: The environment is crucial. Make sure there is nothing to make the singer self-conscious like neighbors, relatives, or anyone nearby that makes them uncomfortable. We want them free to give 100%. Visual aids, aromatic scents, lighting, etc. can be very helpful to get the right mindset for the singer. Sometimes, the room that has the best acoustics does not have the best vibe. I've shown a few singers how to run the multitrack themselves, and let them record in the control room alone, because it produced the best results.

What: What does the singer need to get in the best performance? Ask him or her. I try to have a variety of things on hand for the singer, especially water. Does the vocalist prefer to sit or stand? Do they have a favorite chair or pair of headphones? Think about peripherals: candles, incense, mood lighting, posters, pictures, etc.

Why: I believe that the vocalist is trying to capture an emotion, message, or belief and transfer it to tape. Remember that we're trying to record self-expression. I've seen many sessions ruined because someone lost sight of this goal. Sometimes, having the vocal dissected and analyzed too much compromises the expression of the material. We're not trying to sacrifice the originality of an artist just to fit our own person ideology. We as engineers are there to help, not hinder the process. Remember this, especially if you are both the engineer and the vocalist.

The Headphone Mix

Remember that no matter how good your vocal sound is, the performance is always more important. To this end, the singer needs to be comfortable and happy with the headphone mix. You know how nasty headphones can sound sometimes. They can be too loud and too soft at the same time. It's very unnatural to have music that close to your ears. It's one of the few ways, however, to isolate the music while the singer tracks his/her part. Let me give you a few tips just in case the headphone mix is not happening.

Tip 1: First try a normal headphone mix. The singer has both earphones on, and the music and vocal mix is comparable to a finished song as far as levels. If the singer is unhappy, try changing the levels of the background music. Make it louder or softer depending on the singer's demands. Sometimes, instead of making the music softer, I just remove the low end of the backing tracks going to the headphones. This takes some of the pressure off of the singer's ears and gives them more headroom in the cans (headphones) to fill up and feel big sounding. Be careful with cymbals and guitars as well. They take up a lot of frequency space, and can cause a singer to push to be heard. This should not be necessary in the studio. Just reduce the amount of guitars and cymbals going to the headphone mix.

Tip 2: If this fails, as far as getting happy levels, change the phase on the vocal input at the preamp. The phase symbol looks like a "O" with a line through it (Ø). Here's the idea: The vocalist may be canceling his or her own voice. How? Well, first understand you can have a loss in frequencies whenever you have two identical signals. Their sound waves could be in opposite times of oscillation, causing frequencies to cancel. How are there two identical sounds, you ask? One is coming from their body, throat, and head, and the other is feeding their ears from the headphones. Both sounds are heard by the singer through the ears at the same time. Changing the phase could bring back frequencies that are necessary to clearly hear the vocal with headphones on. It won't, however, change the recorded voice in any way that causes a problem.

Tip 3: If that's not the problem, we go to plan B. Have the singer use only one earphone, leaving their other ear open to the sound of their natural voice. (See photo.)

Please remember to pan the headphone mix into the one side that is on their head. *Don't forget this.* They need to hear all of the music in one earphone, and we need to reduce the amount of noise coming out of the unused side. Panning the headphone mix will get you the desired results.

Tip 4: If none of these are working, ask your singer if they were an only child, spoiled beyond belief. No, seriously, though, let's try another headphone trick.

Sometimes the pressure of headphones causes problems. I'll have the singer slightly pull off the headphones, maybe 1/2"— not enough to cause bleed problems (sound leakage from the headphones into the mic), just enough to remove the pressure off of the ears.

Tip 5: I've found that bulky headphones can sometimes compromise the jaw hinge. The vocalist needs their mouth movement to be uninhibited. You might find that in-ear headphones are the least restricting for this purpose. The singer may feel as if they are not even wearing headphones because these types are so lightweight. The sound quality may not be as good as the kinds that cover the ear, but in this case I'm more interested in comfort than sound quality.

Tip 6: I've recorded vocals without headphones on rare occasions. This means that the singer stands in front of the monitors, directly in the middle. The speakers are then put "out of phase" to cause the sound to go around the center area. The amount of bleed is minimal to tolerable, and feedback is not a problem. (When a stereo sound is put out of phase, it moves away from the center. In this way, the mic doesn't pick up too much bleed.) You need to reverse the polarity on one speaker connection in order to get them to go out of phase. Just remember to put them back in phase when you're mixing.

Tip 7: And last, but not least, try using effects like reverb and delay to monitor with. They can help someone feel more confident—like singing in the shower!—resulting in a better performance. (Of course, it could muddy up the mix and have the singer feeling drowned in their own reflections, too; so don't overdo it.) Generally speaking, a little ambience keeps the singer from feeling claustrophobic in the headphone mix; otherwise, it can sometimes feel like singing in a vacuum (a place with no sound reflections). This could cause the singer to focus too much on listening and not enough on singing.

Comping Vocals

Now that we're going to record the vocals, let's decide upon the best method for you. The first method is called *comping*. When you comp a vocal, you are recording multiple passes, one after the other, and then choosing the best one after they are all done. With a little automation skills, you can pick the best parts of each take, and then join them together to get the best overall performance. Comping allows you to get into the moment, without being responsible for mistakes. What I mean is, it's okay to make some mistakes, because we're only going to keep the best parts later anyway. This doesn't mean that you can sound bad all the time, however. There has to be enough good vocal lines to piece together a good vocal.

How do you decide if you should comp? Number one, it's good for singers who enjoy singing the entire song all the way through. Just make sure the singer has the stamina and technique to sing the song 3 to 10 times in a tracking session. Next, it only works if the singer makes mistakes in different parts of the song each time. If there is a trouble spot, like a high note or hard run, and the singer always messes that part up, then comping won't solve that problem.

Also take in to consideration the amount of tracks you have to record on. If you only have two tracks open for a vocal part, maybe *punching in* would be better. Many times, the vocals are the last thing to be recorded. This means that most of the other tracks are already filled up. If you have three or more open tracks, however, comping is an effective way to get a great sounding vocal.

Last, but not least, is the consideration of improvising. If the vocal part is improvised, which means that the singer is changing the phrasing or wording of the vocal line, then comping is extremely difficult, if not impossible. It's like trying to piece together not just one puzzle, but several different ones at the same time. One line here fits with one line there, but the next line starts too early or ends too late to fit with the next one. Or, the words when joined no longer have the intended meaning. This doesn't mean that you can't experiment and come up with something completely different and exciting, just be aware of the limitations.

If you do decide to comp, you could choose the best words/phrases/lines on a different day than the tracking session. Give the singer and the engineer/producer time away from the song to gain a fresh perspective. If you're tired or unfocused, it's too easy to just pick the lines that sound most correct. The day or so rest allows the singer to get out of singing mode, and into editing mode, with a positive outlook. Just make sure you have enough good material to choose from. The singer won't be able to fix things later without hearing a noticeable difference between the tracking days. The idea was to make it sound like one great vocal take, remember?

Punch-Ins

The other way to fix a vocal is to *punch in* at the mistakes, and replace these parts with better vocal passes. This can be as small as a syllable or large as an entire phrase. If your vocal is good enough without changing anything, then you're not going to need to punch in or comp. I've only had this happen twice in my career. There was always something to fix, no matter how minuscule. The object is to not lose the magic of the performance, though. While comping seems to be the best as far as creating a mood, the fifth or sixth time singing the same song in a row sometimes leaves the singer lifeless. With punching in, you simply record a full pass until you get the most out of the singer. Usually this is within the first few passes. There are a few mistakes, but we will go in and re-record those lines or words one at a time. This leaves something to be desired as far as spontaneity goes, but it gets the job done. This helps the singer in a few ways. One, it allows them to concentrate on the trouble spots. They can be prepared for that high note or difficult passage. Two, it allows them to be rested and fresh when the part comes, instead of always running out of breath at a certain part. And lastly, it allows them to pay attention to detail, to really focus on the little nuances that make up a strong vocal.

In order to punch in a vocal, I recommend that you first have at least two copies of the lyric sheet. The engineer's copy should have *timecode* placed on every line. Timecode is the numbers that appear on your recording device, like a timer-counter. This gives you quick access to the vocal lines. Remember that we want to keep the magic flowing and not give the singer a lot of time to realize that we are unnaturally altering the vocal. We need to keep the same vibe going throughout. No one is supposed to hear the vocal punch-ins. It's supposed to sound like one amazing pass.

Once a vocal take has been recorded that's the best one likely to be done, the singer and engineer need to listen to each line and decide on what words, phrases, etc., need to be re-recorded. I recommend circling these words on the lyric sheet so you know exactly which lines or words are going to be replaced. The singer then goes back into the tracking room, and starts with the first punch-in. The engineer cues up the tape to an appropriate *pre-roll* point before the punch-in. Pre-roll is the amount of time the tape is rewound to, before the punch-in begins. Measuring it in seconds, I usually like about 5 to 8 seconds. Depending on the vocal line length and tempo of the song, this usually translates into one line. This seems to be enough to get the singer prepared for the line, but not too much time, which leads to anxiety and more stress. If the singer is singing along, I like to keep pre-roll to one vocal line so it does not tire them out unnecessarily. When at all possible, it is desirable to have the singer sing along with the track, not just wait to start singing at the punch point. By singing along, the singer creates a natural sounding line when the punch-in occurs. I realize there are times when this is not possible, because of an extremely difficult part, and then it's just hit or miss. In this case, it's up to the engineer to decide whether or not the punch in sounds too obvious, regardless of how good the take was. Again, we're trying to make this seamless.

Would you like an example of an obvious punch-in? Listen to TRACK 33. Can you hear the "glitches" or "pops"? Those are the punching points. The vocal was consistent, but the punching points were not. This created a noticeable problem in the flow of the vocal. In the line "these words long ago," can you hear that the word "long" was from two different passes? It starts one way, and then ends another. Also, the last line "and all the tears…" was slightly cut off at the beginning. This punch was too late, and part of the breath and vocal is missing.

Would you like an example of seamless punching? Take a listen to TRACK 34. How many punch-ins to you hear? Where are they? (See the Answers to Quiz Questions page.) In order to create seamless punching, there are a few guidelines that I'd like you to follow:

- The best place to punch in is during silence. Today's modern digital recorders (or professional analog) leave no punching noises by themselves. You know the noises I'm referring to, from when you used a hand-held cassette recorder. Any time you pressed the record button, it made a loud click or thump, and left a short gap on the tape. Well, not with good multitrack recorders. Whenever possible, punch in and out during space on the vocal, like in between lines and words. Just be careful to listen for breathing. Breathing is still sound on the tape. Punch in/out before or after the breath, wherever you have more time.

- If you are unable to punch in/out in a space, choose the very beginning of an attack. For a vocal, choose the beginning of a word with a consonant—words like try, buy, go, etc. Because it's the beginning of a new sound, it's hard for the audience to know how the word was actually started. So if the color changes, only the singer/engineer know. Listen to TRACK 35. Where did I punch in? I punched in on the word "told." Notice how seamless the punch-in point was? That's what you're aiming for.

- As a last resort to re-doing the entire line again, you can try punching-in syllables. These are the parts of the word, within the word. Let's use "already" as an example. Already can be broken into three parts: al-rea-dy. If the part of the word "rea" is pitchy (meaning there's some kind of pitch problem) we could try to replace it with a punch-in. The trick is not to erase the first or last syllable while doing it. In these cases, I prefer to use the auto-punch feature on my recorder. I'll locate the end of the syllable "al" and the beginning of the syllable "dy." When I've found the right points, the word will have a perfect space between "al" and "dy." There will be no remains of the syllable "rea." In rehearsal mode on a recorder, you can listen to your punch-in and -out points without erasing material. I'll adjust these points until I get it perfect. The hardest part is now up to the singer. It's their job to phrase the line the same way in order to fill in the space perfectly.

If you have a computer with waveform editing, your job is easier, and you have other options available to you. You can have the singer repeat the line several times, and just cut and paste the one that works. I've been trying to give advice to the people who do not have unlimited tracks, and no visual guide to help them along.

Doubling a Lead Vocal

Another method of helping a vocal in need is *doubling*. Doubling is when you record the same vocal twice, and use both when listening back. If the singer is not capable of or does not wish to fix the little mistakes, doubling can mask them. It creates a natural chorus at the points where the pitch is slightly different. It can actually be better than using a chorus effects processor (see next chapter), because the singer's pitch can change in both directions up and down. Most chorus devices work on a detune principal that only allows the vocals to go flat. This would be bad on a singer that is already flat in most spots. It would exaggerate the problem, not hide it.

Doubling also helps a weaker voice sound fuller. It fills up more space in the mix and supports the initial track. It works nice on falsetto notes, or entire phrases. Pitch and phrasing are very important, however. The double needs to be as close to the first recording as possible. You can double at the same pitch or even an octave down, to help the vocal increase in mass. Just make sure that the intonation and phrasing are as identical as possible. This includes vibrato. Most doubled parts that work well either lack vibrato altogether or the singer can duplicate it effortlessly. Having a double with different vibratos is basically just annoying.

Here's an example of a vocal that could use some help (TRACK 36). If you wanted to thicken it up a bit, doubling might be an option. Let's listen to how doubling helps this vocal (TRACK 37). These are two weak vocal lines playing back at the same time. They are panned only slightly—about 10 o'clock and 2 o'clock in the panning spectrum—in order to remove phase shifting (when two or more like signals cycle at opposite degrees and end up partially cancelling each other out). Consider using doubling instead of pushing the singer, when they have a naturally soft or weak voice, and you think the track needs a stronger vocal line.

Background Vocals

Background vocals exist to complement the lead vocal line. They can do this in many ways. Harmonies are an excellent example of helping the vocal melody, within the context of the chord progression going on behind it. "Gang" or "group" chorus voices help fill up more space to provide big accents. Call-and-response style backgrounds help fill up space between the singer's lines for continuity and phrasing ideas. Whatever type of backing vocals you are recording, the goal is to remember that the backing vocals are there to support the main vocal. We don't want them detracting from the lead vocalist.

When backgrounds are well arranged and properly sung, they need only a little help from the engineer. There is a completely different vocal technique for background singing. The approach focuses on blending with the main vocal, and is a pleasant experience for almost every engineer/producer. However, not all singers are skilled in lead vocal technique, much less background vocal technique. So let's learn to deal with making amateur background vocals sound as good as they can.

Blending with EQ

Being a background vocalist is an art form unto itself. Just like playing lead and rhythm guitar can be opposite challenges, so can vocals and backing vocals. One of the main problems with backing vocals is their tendency to overpower the main vocal. If this were the problem, I would start by removing some low to low-mids on the EQ. This will thin them out, just enough to allow the main vocals to appear richer. One main vocal track against several powerful back vocal tracks is not a fair competition. I'd still like to have the back vocals loud, just not so greedy in terms of sonic space. Removing between 100Hz and 400Hz could help your problem.

Listen to TRACK 38. This is a full music example with one vocal line (no effects). Now listen to TRACK 39. This is the same as TRACK 38, except with one back vocal line added in. The back vocal is a full voice part. This means that it has not been sung as a background part. Notice how it does not blend in with the main vocal. They tend to clash, because they are both trying to be lead lines. Listen to TRACK 40. With a little help from an EQ, I've blended it in better. I haven't changed the levels; I've removed certain frequencies that were too powerful for a background voice. I've removed about 8 decibels of 300Hz (wide bandwidth) and 8 decibels of 3kHz (medium bandwidth). Taking out 300Hz removed some of the "power" of the background voice, and removing the 3kHz range reduced the "bite" or "attack" in order to smooth it out and blend better.

Doubling or Tripling

Another problem is just the opposite of the last example. What do you do when the background vocal part sounds weak and thin? I'm going to show you what happens when you double and/or triple these parts. Remember that doubling will add fullness to almost any vocal sound. When doubling or tripling a part, just make sure that the takes are as tight as possible. Take a listen to TRACK 41. This background line sounds like it just isn't going to work. By itself, it sounds weak, thin, and almost unusable. But it can still be salvaged. Listen to TRACK 42. This example has the same line sung three times. Each voice by itself is still thin and weak. But when they are put together, they smooth each other out and thicken up. Just imagine throwing on some harmonies as well...

The point is not to give up on anything, until you've tried every tool you have available. And remember, we haven't even reached the section on effects yet. The possibilities are almost limitless.

"Flying-In" Parts

If you're using a digital recording system that allows you to do cut-and-paste editing, then you may be interested in flying-in vocal parts, especially backing vocals. While it does remove the ability for phrasing nuances, it helps when time is limited (or running out) or the vocalist is unable to sing the part two or three more times. Remember that the human voice has its limitations, and even though you might have time for more recording, the vocalist might not be able to continue. Take for example a chorus line that repeats the same melody, and that happens three times in the song. If the line is identical in all three choruses, all you need is one good line. Then you simply copy that one to each part in the song. Again, this is done to save time and remedy the problem of a singer who doesn't have the vocal stamina to sing the part over and over again. Many times, I'm left with a burned-out singer when it comes time for backing vocals, or no money left in the budget for additional tracking time.

You have to use your ears, in order to make sure that when you copy the part, it ends up in the right timing. If you're using a computer, you can move everything by numbers, so there is no chance for error.

I've also used this concept for tracking the lead vocal, with a twist. When the singer was having trouble with a specific line in a verse, I just had her sing it over and over, instead of going to the next line. When we listened back, we heard one good line out of the five or so repetitions, and simply cut and pasted it back where it belonged in the verse. Then we continued along with the rest of the lines. This works when the chord progression repeats itself. It doesn't matter whether the vocalist gets it on the first round or the second, because I can just paste it wherever I want, once I get a good take. Think about the possibilities of "flying-in" parts in order to help the singer get the best performance he/she can.

Effects

Okay, some of you have skipped the other sections and jumped right to this one! So let me state first that I believe effects should be monitored, but not tracked, whenever possible. Either set them up by using effect sends for a headphone mix, or print them during the mixdown. The amount of vocal effects you use while tracking is almost always different when it comes to mixing. If you record your vocal effects during tracking, you will be locking yourself into a setting that you can't undo later.

With that said, there are three categories of effects that I'm going to discuss: space-based, time-based, and pitch-based. The three effects that fill those categories are reverb, delay, and chorus, respectively. I'm also going to show you how to use a gate to get rid of unwanted noise, and how to use a pitch corrector if the vocalist's intonation is off.

Let's start with spatial effects like reverb...

Reverb

Many singers (and engineers) are uncomfortable with the sound of a person's voice miked up at close range and dead dry. I admit, with some singers, it's awkward to listen to. One justifiable reason for using effects is to put the room ambience back into the vocal sound. It's very unnatural to listen to sounds without some type of ambience or reflections. Reverbs are used to simulate the reflections of the signal caused by surrounding surface areas—a bathroom, a closet, an auditorium, a basement, etc. Reverbs have three main categories: rooms, halls, and plates.

Room: Room reverb is the easiest to relate with. We hear it every day. Whenever you're in an enclosed space that's not particularly big, you're in a room. Room reverbs have a sound that is very natural to the original source (in this case, the vocal). Let's listen to a typical room reverb on a vocal. First listen to the dry vocal on TRACK 43. Now, listen to the vocal with a small room reverb on TRACK 44. Notice how the vocal fills up more space in TRACK 44, due to the reverb. Now listen to just the reverb by itself on TRACK 45. This is what the reverb is adding to the dry vocal take. Notice how the reverb sound is slightly different from the dry vocal sound. It sounds like the dry vocal take, but placed farther away from the microphone, a bit darker, and with the reflections from the walls added in.

Room reverbs retain clarity better than plate and hall settings. They give the feeling of depth, but not unnaturally. They are often found as stereo sounds and therefore add size to the vocal part. This makes the vocal sound "bigger." Again, it's a very natural quality to listen to. It does not distract from the vocal line. When the words need to be ultra clear, the tempo is fast, or you're just not a big fan of effected vocals, a room reverb can help the vocal fit comfortably with the rest of the music.

If you've been listening to the previous CD examples, you'll notice that none of the vocal parts have reverb on them. I did this on purpose in order to isolate the specific topics that I've been talking about. So, you should already be familiar with the sound of "dry" vocals. However, to have a point of reference, listen to TRACK 46. This is a music example with a dry vocal. It sounds in the "front" of the mix and narrow as far as space is concerned. Now listen to TRACK 47. I've added room reverb this time. Notice how the vocal gets "wider" because the reverb allows the vocal sound to take more space. It also takes it out of the front of the mix, so it doesn't stick out as much. Because we're using a room reverb, the vocal won't go too far back in the mix. It only adds a little depth.

Hall: Next are the hall reverbs. Halls are much larger areas. The reflections take longer to develop and come back at varying times. Unlike the room reverb that was short and tight, the hall reverb is longer and less clear sounding. Listen to the dry vocal again on TRACK 43. Now here is the same vocal with a large hall reverb (TRACK 48). And now listen to just the hall reverb (TRACK 49). Notice how different the dry vocal and the effected sound are. The hall is not tight sounding. It has many reflections that "mask" or cover up the vocal. You can hear how one word runs into the next. Halls are useful on ballads and slow tempo music with lots of space. The hall reverb gives a more bombastic quality to the vocal. It helps the listener to imagine hearing the singer in a big setting. While room reverbs were more intimate sounding, the halls have a more distanced feel to them. Remember that reverb has the ability to create an environment that wasn't available at the tracking session. Sometimes visualizing where the vocal would best be sung can help in your choosing of the right type of reverb for the part.

Plate: Lastly is plate reverb. Plates have qualities of both rooms and halls with a bit of their own added in. The unique part about plate reverb is its metallic reflections. Plate reverbs are very bright sounding. This is due to the simulation of reflections off of a metal surface. They are initially long in duration, kind of like halls. So, you get a longer reverb that has a sizzling sound that stays bright, but not too clear—kind of like a hall and room, but uniquely its own sound. Let's listen: first, to the dry vocal again (TRACK 43), and then the same vocal with plate reverb (TRACK 50). And now, just the plate reverb by itself, so you can hear what it's adding to the vocal (TRACK 51). Notice how sibilant the reverb becomes on "s" sounds. Plate reverbs are very rich sounding and fill up lots of space. Again, they're good on slower-tempo songs, or vocals that are very sparse. They're not very intimate sounding but can fit well into an appropriate mix (TRACK 52). They tend to sound "airy," so they work well on many ballads and songs desiring bright vocal sounds.

I know that you don't want to hear this, but... Reverb is a matter of opinion. Everyone has their own needs and desires of what they want to hear. My recommendation is to listen to CDs that have vocal sounds that you like, and try to figure out which of the three reverbs (room, hall, or plate) was used. Sometimes, the vocal has none. Sometimes, they use more than one. That's why I gave you the examples of the reverbs by themselves, so you can learn to distinguish one from the other. This is part of your ear training exercises, which I recommend you work on every day. Just like a singer or guitarist practices scales, you need to work on identifying sounds.

My biggest "ear-opener" was when I learned to put a CD player "out of phase." What this did was cancel out anything in the center of the stereo field, and allow me to hear much more clearly what type of effects they were using (as long as they were panned). Basically, what I did was run the CD outputs into two channels of my console and send each channel to both speakers. The CD was now running in mono from two channels. I then flipped the phase on one of the channels using a phase button (it is a Greek symbol called "theta" that looks like this: Ø). This shifted the phase of one channel, causing all of the center to drop out. Since that is where the vocal is most often, what was left of the vocal was mainly effect. If you have a "karaoke" setting on your CD player, you can use that to get an idea of stereo phase cancellation. Otherwise (unless you have access to a console with phase reversal switches on the input channels), you're going to have to listen very carefully. Practice and experiment as much as you can, and try to learn from your mistakes.

In order to find just the right reverb sound, you may need to adjust or "tweak" a few parameters. The ones that I want to discuss affect the length, brightness, and placement of the reverb. These three parameters will greatly add to your ability to custom tailor a reverb to your individual mix and to choose the most appropriate space in which to put your vocal.

Decay/Time

This parameter can go by many different names like decay, length, time, etc. I believe "decay" and "time" are the most commonly used terms. This parameter adjusts the overall length of the reflections and is measured in milliseconds. With this parameter, you can extend a room into the size of a hall. A general time setting for a room is less than 500 milliseconds. A hall starts somewhere around 1000 milliseconds. Most plates have long preset times around 2000 milliseconds. Does this mean that these are the times you have to use? No way, not if your effect unit has an adjustable time/decay setting. Some effects units have preset parameters that cannot be altered. Hopefully, you have a device that has adjustable settings for time.

Let's listen to the difference between shorter and longer decay settings. Do you remember when I mentioned earlier that plate reverbs had long initial settings? Most of the time, people get scared off by this preset and avoid plate reverbs altogether. When I was loading in plate reverbs from my Lexicon unit, here was the initial setting (TRACK 53). This is a big, spacious plate reverb. I liked the texture of the reverb; I just wanted it to be shorter. Listen to TRACK 54. After adjusting the decay time, this is what I ended up using. The reverb is still the same volume as the initial settings; it's just shorter, so it appears like less reverb. Because of the phrasing in my vocal example, I found the time setting (1070 milliseconds) to be more appropriate than the factory preset of 2.36 seconds. This way, the reverb ends before each new phrase begins, which keeps the vocal from sounding muddy.

Again, it's a matter of being very particular for each song, without getting locked into generalizations. I'm hoping that if you better understand these parameters, you can alter the factory presets to better suit your needs.

High Frequency Cut-Off (HFC)

HFC also has many different names depending on the reverb unit you're using. Some may say "brightness" with a percentage setting, others may say "low pass filter" with a frequency choice. Any way you look at it, this parameter is trying to reduce unwanted top end from the reverb. HFC determines which frequencies are able to pass through the unit when it's generating the reverb. By selecting a frequency, let's say 10kHz, you are telling the unit not to allow any frequencies higher than 10,000Hz to come out. You are filtering those frequencies out, or cutting them off, hence the names. Listen: it's okay to have a bright vocal sound, but not always a bright reverb. It's like painting a sign in your mix that says, "Hey, look at me!!! I'm the reverb!" Sometimes it's cool to have reverb that's subtle in its effectiveness. In order to make a large reverb not stick out like a sore thumb, you may need to darken the verb. Again, I don't want to darken the vocal, and thereby make it unclear. I just want to warm up the verb by removing some of the shrillness associated with certain frequencies.

Let's listen to TRACK 55. Notice how much "color" the reverb has. It's very "present" sounding, and the "s" and "t" consonants jump out. Now listen to TRACK 56. This is with the HFC set at 4kHz. There is still just as much reverb, just without 4kHz (and above) in the reverb. In this way, you can use generous amounts of reverb without the listener becoming aware of how much you're using.

Of course, you can always just turn the amount of reverb down, if that's what is necessary; I'm just trying to give you different ways to decrease the perception of reverb, without altering the amount being used.

Predelay

Last but not least is the ability to offset when the reverb begins. You thought it started instantly all the time? No. You have the ability to alter when the reverb starts if you have a predelay setting.

In order to understand this setting, and how it affects the listener's perception, imagine yourself at a big concert. Imagine there are three places you can sit in order to watch the show. The first is the back row. By the time the band's sound is projected through the main speakers and to your ears, it has bounced off of every wall and surface in the place (except the back wall). You are hearing a blend of the dry signal and the reverb at the same time. The sound would be pretty unclear, with the reverb blending in with the original source. There is little or no delay between the two sounds.

What happens when you move to the middle of the auditorium? You would hear the sound slightly before the majority of the reverb returns off of the walls. The band would sound clearer and the reverb would help add ambience to the sound. There is a slight predelay, or delay before the reverb, in which you hear the signal dry (i.e., without effect), and then the effect comes in behind it.

The last is the front row. How much reverb will you hear if you are right in front of the band? Not much, compared to the dry sound coming off of the stage. And when you do hear the reflections they will be noticeably later than the original sound. The band would be very clear, and the reverb would be noticed mainly in the pauses between the sound. This has a huge predelay that can sometimes sound like a slapback. If you've ever played on stage in a big room, you'll understand what I'm talking about.

Anyway, predelay is used to "pause" the reverb in order to let the original sound retain clarity. It sounds unnatural when listened to by itself, but when placed in the mix, it's amazing how the vocal will cut through. Listen to TRACK 57, a reverbed vocal with no predelay. Notice how easy it is to have the reverb sound like a cavern. There is a 0 setting on the predelay in this example, so the mix between the wet and dry sound is instantaneous. Now listen to TRACK 58. This is the same reverb with a predelay of 80ms. Because I've increased the predelay, I've also decreased the decay time. The reverb still ends at the same time in both examples, it just starts later in the last example. In TRACK 58, the vocal has a chance to separate from the reverb, due to the predelay. It's subtle, but very effective in a mix.

What I'm trying to do with these parameter settings is show you that the descriptions "too much" or "not enough" reverb are rarely an accurate description. The next time you feel you need more or less reverb, before you simply adjust the volume of the effect, make sure that you have the right reverb and that the parameters are adjusted to suit your needs.

Delay

The next effect I'd like to introduce is delay. Delay allows the user to repeat the exact word or phrase, later in time. Depending upon the settings, you can get sustain effects, slapback, stereo panning, or echoes. I think the object of using delay is to get the effect to fill in between the spaces in the vocal phrasing. It will help make the vocal sound "bigger" without getting muddy or dark or falling too far back in the mix.

You've heard delay in a natural setting before, if you've ever been to the Grand Canyon or a large amphitheater. Unfortunately, you've also heard reverb blended in at the same time. If you've heard an entire word or phrase repeat after you've said them, then you've experienced delay. The fact that the sound also reflected off various surfaces at different times, and made the echo sound far away, is the reverb part. In the studio, delay is separate from reverb. You can use both effects at the same time, and in fact, it's so popular that I've included it in this chapter.

First, let's just listen to what delay sounds like on a vocal. First, without the effect (TRACK 43). Now, the same example with delay (TRACK 59). It's the exact same sound, just later in time (by 300ms). The delay helps fill out the vocal, but unlike reverb (which gives the sound depth), the vocal remains upfront and clear. Take a listen to TRACK 60, and compare this delay effect with TRACK 52, which has plate reverb. Notice the difference?

As with reverb, the presets in most effects units are great starting points, but they can be customized to your specifications. There are two delay parameters you can adjust that I'd like to discuss here: time and feedback.

Time

The time parameter is usually measured in milliseconds, although some units have measurements in rhythmic dictation against a bpm reading. Let's start with milliseconds. 1000 milliseconds is the same as one second. This means that the repetitions start one second after input is received, and are spaced one second apart every time they repeat. 500 milliseconds is 1/2 second, 250 is 1/4, and so on.

Milliseconds are difficult to judge in terms of the tempo of the song. You can use a formula to figure out what one quarter note (or one beat) is worth in milliseconds, as long as you know the beats per minute (bpm) of the song. 60 bpm means one beat per second, so 1000 milliseconds would be one quarter note in time. 500 milliseconds would be an eighth note, and 250 would be a sixteenth note. Let's take 70 bpm as a tougher example. Divide 60 by the tempo (in this case, the tempo is 70), and that will give you how many thousands of milliseconds equals one quarter note. So, 60/70 = .857. This means 857 milliseconds will give me a quarter-note delay. Half of that, or 428, will give me an eighth-note delay. Numbers with fractions are a pain, so just round up or down accordingly. Here's the formula:

$$60 \div tempo = \text{thousands of milliseconds}$$

Having done all that work, you may find that your delay unit let's you input the tempo (bpm) and the type of note you want (quarter note, triplet, etc.). Well, then there's no math to do. Happy day! Or your unit might have a "tap tempo" display. In this case, you just listen to the music, and tap in the type of delay you want (quarter note, triplet, eighth note, etc.). You just need to tap twice, once for the start time and once for the end time. The delay unit calculates the time between taps, and inputs that setting.

So, what delay time setting are you going to use? Well, first try picking a time that is not the most commonly used within the singer's phrasing. If the singer sings a lot of eighth notes, an eighth-note delay will either be buried in the other words, or harmonize randomly (and usually not pleasantly). I use a lot of quarter-note triplets (3/2) for this reason. They're usually not consistent phrasing rhythms, and the delay falls nicely between the other notes being sung. Sometimes I'll just pick a random number in the 300's that isn't in any easily recognizable time. This assures that the delay won't be identical to the phrasing of the singer.

In general, however, tempo and vocal phrasing affect the time setting most. Slower tempos need longer time settings, and vocals that are spaced closer together need shorter ones.

Feedback

This could also be called "repeats" on your delay unit. Feedback (or repeats) determines how many times the delay will occur. If you're lucky enough to have a "repeats" setting, then the math is easy. A setting of one equals one repeat, two = two, etc. However, if you have "feedback," it's a percentage reading. The percentage applies to the maximum ability of your unit (up to infinite). Each time the delay repeats, it decreases in volume until it disappears. For an example, listen to TRACK 61. This is a 3% feedback setting. There is the original word "find," and then the delay repeats it two more times until it fades away. Depending on how loud you have your CD player turned up, you should hear one strong repeat (after the initial word) and one weaker repeat. In TRACK 62, the feedback setting is at 15%. How many times do you hear the repeat? Don't count the first "find" because that's the original dry vocal. Again, because it's a percentage of volume reading, the loudness of your playback system may affect your answer. (For the answer, see Answers to Quiz Questions at the end of the book.)

Stereo Delay

Okay, so you've heard TRACK 60, which has a standard delay on the vocal. Let's take another example called stereo delay. I'm going to take the vocal and process it with a stereo delay setting. This means that the delay time is going to be very short (between 15 and 60ms), and the feedback will be at 0%. At 0%, I will get only one repeat. Next, I'll pan the original vocal to one side (left) and the effect to the other side (right). This is going to spread the vocal sound out across the entire stereo spectrum. Why put the delay on it? Let me show you what happens to two identical sounds panned left and right. Listen to TRACK 63. This is the dry vocal on the left and the delay in bypass mode, panned to the right. It's basically the exact same signals, panned to each side. Put on a pair of headphones, and take a listen to where the vocal appears. It appears in the center! Yes that's right, in the center. When two equal sounds are panned to the left and right sides they end up in the middle. However, if there is a slight difference in time (or tone), the sounds will appear in the right and left, not the center. Listen to TRACK 64. This is a delay setting of 40ms on the right side, and the dry vocal on the left. Notice how you can hear the vocal out of the left and right sides. It does not appear in the middle. Go back to TRACK 63 and compare again. Which one sounds wider and bigger to you? Of course, TRACK 64. It occupies more space, without reverb and without an echo effect. What does it sound like in a mix? Listen to TRACK 65 for an example. Try this out on your vocal the next time standard delay or reverb is not happening.

Delay with Reverb

One thing that may be undesirable about delay is that it is not very subtle. It's not just a matter of how loud it is in the mix either; it sometimes sounds too direct or "up front." So one of the things I like to do, to "soften" up the delay effect, is to feed it into a reverb, before it returns to the mixer. You can "daisy chain" these two effects, if they are found in two different units, or you can simply put them in the order of delay-reverb, if you have a multi-effects device. This will allow the delay to have depth or space in the mix, and not sit right in the front of the speakers.

Let's listen to what the delay/reverb effect sounds like with a vocal (TRACK 66). Notice how the repeats are not as clear and up front as TRACK 61. The original vocal is still in the front of the mix, but the delay is now washing out in the background, giving a nice, subtle delay effect. Let's listen to this same vocal in context of a mix (TRACK 67). Compare this with TRACK 52, TRACK 60, and TRACK 65. I've purposefully been using the exact same vocal line for every example so you can compare the different effects, in order for you to be able judge what you would use.

Chorus

Another effect you might choose is chorus. Chorus, like the name implies, will thicken a vocal part by simulating another voice or voices, slightly different than the original. It is different from stereo delay because it slightly alters the pitch of the original vocal.

Natural chorus happens when you attempt to double or triple a musical phrase. It's almost impossible to have the exact same timing and pitch when the performance is repeated. These small discrepancies (and I do mean small) create a natural chorus, or sound of multiple voices. The timing is slightly different, and the pitch is close, but not perfect; But these differences allow the vocal (or any other musical sound) to fill up more space in the audio spectrum. The differences cannot be so much that the performances sound off when listening to them all at once.

A chorus device is an artificial way to double a vocal line. You won't need to sing the part again, and therefore you don't have to worry about doubling your vibrato exactly, or trying to duplicate your tone and/or phrasing. Let's listen to an example of chorus on a vocal line (TRACK 68). Notice how it sounds like there is more than one of the same voice. The stereo chorus is panned left and right, and thickens and widens the original vocal sound. There are two main parameters in a chorus effect: depth and rate.

Depth

Depth will determine how far out-of-tune the effected vocal sound will be in relation to the original vocal pitch. Sometimes it's measured in percentages; other times, in cents. The idea is to not have so small of a setting that the effect turns into a phaser, but not so much that the vocal sounds "underwater" or out of tune. Here are both examples of what not to do: TRACK 69 is an example of too much depth. Notice how the vocal sounds like it is going in and out of tune? And TRACK 70, which is too little depth, which turns into a bad phaser effect.

Rate

Did you notice that the depth modulates, or changes back to the original pitch, after reaching its deepest point? The other parameter, rate (or time), controls how quickly it modulates. It can be measured in Hertz or milliseconds. The higher the time value, the more "water-like" (with a lot of depth) or "wavy" (with less depth) the chorus sounds. You might wish to set the rate so that it is in time with the music. Just decide whether you want it to be noticeable or not. Slower rates are harder to hear than quicker ones. Here's an example of chorus in the context of a mix (TRACK 71). Compare this example to TRACK 46, in order to hear how much wider the vocal is, in relation to the dry vocal mix.

I recommend using the chorus in stereo. In other words, your vocal is probably mixed in the center of your music, and I would put the chorus off to the left and right sides of the panning spectrum. You'll need to use a stereo chorus that has two outputs in order to do this properly. Again, the purpose of using the chorus is to help a weaker or thinner voice. By adding the chorus, we fill up more space in the music, and the vocal will appear bigger.

Okay, so now you have a bunch of different effects and examples of each to get you going. There is almost an unlimited amount of effects you could use if you wanted to get weird with the vocal. These I will leave to you, in order to experiment until you go crazy.

Using a Noise Gate

Because you're probably not recording in an acoustically treated, soundproof room, you might need to use a noise gate. Do you hear humming or buzzes, neighbors, dogs, cars, or other noises while you're recording? If you're using a condenser microphone and a compressor, you'll be amazed at what gets recorded along with your vocal. Take a listen to TRACK 72. Do you hear the radio voices in the background? That sound was in the next room while I was tracking. I did this on purpose, just so you would be aware of the potential problems of recording in your environment. Normally, I would make sure that there were no other sounds going on while I was recording. But you might not have control over your neighbors, traffic, pets, etc. I'm going to show you how to use a gate to get rid of these noises.

I'm just going to recommend that you use the noise gate after you're done recording. Why, you ask? Because if you set the parameters wrong, you could erase parts of the vocal, and that would be a mistake you can't undo. If you use the gate after you record (during the mixdown), then you have the option to continually adjust the settings as you go, without permanently erasing the vocal.

Listen to TRACK 73, which uses a gate to get rid of the noise, without compromising the vocal track. If you're listening very critically, you'll hear a little noise "bleeding" through at the very end. It's a minimal problem, but it shows the limitations of the gate. Again, I do not want to mess up the vocal by using the gates. Gates are supposed to be discrete, or unnoticeable to the listener. So what are the limitations of the gate? Here they are:

- The unwanted noise has to be lower in volume than all the wanted vocal sounds.
- The unwanted noise has to happen before or after the wanted sounds occur.

In other words, the gate is just a sonic door that opens and closes. When the door opens, everything comes through. When the door is shut, everything is muted. It doesn't remove the noise, it just mutes the track depending upon the settings you apply.

Threshold

The first gate setting is *threshold*. This determines where (in volume or decibels) the gate turns on and off. This level has to be lower than the softest vocal part, including the beginning and ending of every word. But it needs to be higher than the loudest unwanted background noise. As long as you have a clear difference between the two levels, then you can find the proper threshold setting.

Let me give you an example of a threshold setting that is too low. Listen to TRACK 74. It's the same as TRACK 73, but my threshold is set 12dB lower than before. Notice how some of the noise is coming through. Because the threshold is too low, some of the noise qualifies as being loud enough to open the door. This makes the gate less effective. How about if it's too effective? Here is a threshold setting that is too high (TRACK 75). Notice how some of the beginnings of the words are missing the first letter, like "good" and "try"? Or did you notice that the word "to" was missing at the end? This is not an acceptable threshold setting either. The proper setting removes the noise but not any of the vocal.

Range

The next setting is *range* or mute depth. This determines how quiet the background noise becomes when the gate is closed. Think of the gate as a door. When the door closes, how much sound disappears? The thicker the door, the more the sound goes away. In other words, the higher the range setting, the more effective the gate becomes against the background noise.

Here's an example where the range is not set high enough (TRACK 76), and even though the gate is closed, the noise still gets through. The range setting is -8dB. This means that even when the gate is closed, it will only block out 8 decibels of noise. Anything above 8 decibels "bleeds" through the closed gate. It's like a bad apartment building where you can hear your neighbors, even though there's a wall between you. When the "door" closes, you want the noise to go away. How much range does it take to make the noise go away? Just gradually increase your range setting until the noise is no longer heard. Depending on the amount of background noise you have, you'll need to adjust your range accordingly.

Release/Decay

The *release* or *decay* is the last setting. Release allows the gate time to close, so that it doesn't cut off the ends of the wanted sounds, in this case, the ends of the words. It's like a door gradually closing. Imagine an automatic door at the grocery store: after you pass through the door, it slowly closes; it doesn't slam shut the instant you cross the threshold. In music, the vocal needs time to sustain after it has dropped below the threshold of the gate.

Do you understand that the threshold you set earlier is based upon the attack, or the beginning of the vocal? In almost all sounds, there is a level difference between the attack and sustain of the sound, with the sustain being lower in volume. So what happens after the attack is done and the vocal sustains? The gate begins to close, and depending upon the release setting, it either closes before or after the vocal finishes.

Do you know what it sounds like if the gate closes before the vocal is finished? Here's an example of a release time that is too short (TRACK 77). Do you notice how the ends of some words like "look" and "out" get cut off? On the other hand, if the release is too long, the unwanted noises "sneak" in through the door while it's closing (TRACK 78).

Just remember that the analogy of the door is fairly accurate. This means that while the door is open for the vocal to come through, everything else can come through at this time too. The gate is not filtering out frequencies. It's either on (and blocking sound), or it's off and all sounds come through.

Gating gets a really bad reputation in the engineering world. If you set it wrong in any of the parameters, you can destroy a good vocal part. How do you avoid doing this? Just don't set it wrong! Listen to the vocal after it's been gated to make sure that none of the words have been compromised. If you can't seem to get it right, then don't use it. Gates are like guns. Guns don't kill people. People with guns kill people. Gates don't kill sound. Bad engineers with gates kill sound.

Using an Auto-Tuner

One of the more recent inventions in the world of vocals is the *auto-tuner*. While I believe in having the vocalist work towards getting the best performance first, there are many times when a pitch corrector comes in handy. An auto-tuner or pitch corrector can take single-note lines and adjust them to the nearest pitch in any given key or scale. For me, it's unpleasant to listen to a vocalist when their intonation is off. It just doesn't sound professional. The singer doesn't have to be perfect like a robot, but it shouldn't sound like something's wrong with the vocal. Drummers are expected to have a groove with time, and singers are expected to have a feel with pitch.

I'm not talking about completely missing the notes, I'm talking about the intonation when the note is sounded. I'm very sympathetic towards the demands of a vocal. Unlike a piano or guitar, a vocalist doesn't just press a key or find a fret. So while they might be hitting an "A," the cents (fine-tune measurement of pitch) might be a little off. The engineer/producer should be most concerned about the delivery and the emotional connection the singer is delivering. If the pitch corrector can aid an unprofessional singer who would otherwise need years of experience to nail it just right, then I'll use it. (I just have a moral dilemma with using the device as a crutch, or permanent excuse not to correct vocal problems. It's okay as a temporary solution when "time is money," but I don't want to see the music world turn into a bunch of untalented non-musicians who have the budget to fake what real musicians should be able to do... Sorry about the tirade.)

Getting back to using the pitch corrector, first understand that you need to be nearer to the desired note than to any other note. The auto-tuner adjusts to the nearest note in either direction, up or down. Second, you can set the device to be chromatic or diatonic, so know all the notes that the singer is going to need corrected, and select the appropriate scale or key. Third, the device has a speed at which it reacts to the incoming signals. The faster the speed, the more accurate and the more machine-like the effect will sound. The slower the speed, the more natural the effect, but you run the risk of not correcting notes in time. Lastly, watch out with vibrato, as the machine tends to quantize the natural pitch change of the voice during vibrato, if your settings are too intense.

Okay, here's an example of a vocal that needs to be closer in pitch/intonation (TRACK 79). Listen especially at the end to the word "truth." The pitch is flat compared to the guitars and keyboards in the mix. For me, it's totally embarrassing. Depending on how accurate your ability to hear pitch is, you'll either not notice that it's off, or cringe/laugh every time you listen to it. If you're somewhere near the laugh or cringe category, then take a listen to TRACK 80. This is the same vocal run through the Antares auto-tuner. Notice how the word "truth" smoothly transitions to the appropriate pitch changes. Take a look at the following snapshot of my computer screen to see the settings that I used.

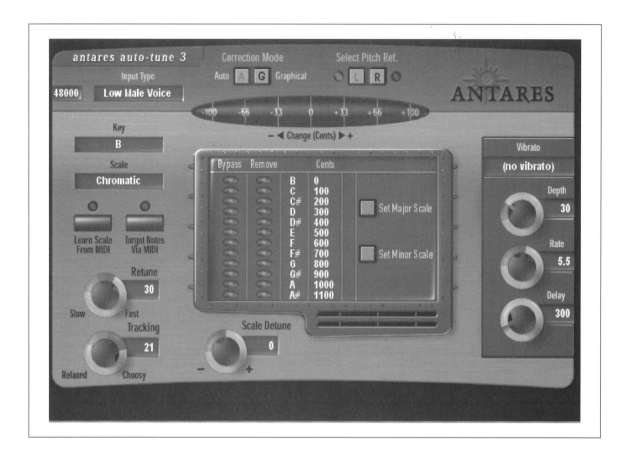

The "retune" affects how quickly the notes are changed, and the "tracking" helps decide which notes are corrected and which are left alone. I've chosen the key of "B," but I've also chosen "chromatic" because there is a key change from the verse to the chorus.

It's important to experiment with the settings and treat each song individually. I don't use the auto-tuner while I'm recording; I use it while mixing, so I don't have to worry about it being destructive (i.e., permanently changing the recorded sound). I try to use the processor as discretely as possible. Remember that I'm trying to get the results of what a more talented vocalist could do, without anyone realizing that the vocal has been altered in any way.

For some styles of music, a pitch corrector might be inappropriate, because of the desire for a "raw" or "unpolished" sound. Remember, I'm just giving you the tools, and it's your choice to use them or not.

Closing

I hope this book/CD has helped answer questions you've had about recording vocals, as well as inspired you with new ideas. Re-read the different sections as many times as you wish—you never know what you'll pick up each time.

Knowledge comes to those who seek it, but at its own pace. I wish you peace and success in all your recording adventures.

—**Dallan Beck**

Acknowledgments

Written and engineered by: Dallan Beck

Original music by: Dallan Beck

Recorded on PRO-TOOLS

Photography by: Tevis Sauer Karlsson

Product support from: Karl W. Winkler at Neumann, Brad Zell at Avalon Design, and Andy Clark at Lexicon

Career support from: John Beck, Jennifer and Jim Hancock, T.J. Helmerich, Dolores and Verner Hoaglund, Wade Gunkel, Ron Connely, Don Beck, Pete Kacinskas, and Alice and Bob Skewis

Thanks to: Hila Calif, Rick Silva, Orlando Rashid, Mark Goodman, Michael Logue at Antares Audio, and Kyle (KJ) Hancock at CoolNephew.com

A special thanks to Jeff Schroedl, Doug Downing, and everyone at Hal Leonard Corporation.

Index

Microphones

Track

1-3   Listening to different microphones

4   Rumble noise

5   Rumble removed with roll-off

6   Sweet spot

7   Vocal with proximity effect

8   Vocal without proximity effect

Compression

9   Uncompressed vocal in music

10   Compressed vocal in music

11   Uncompressed vocal by itself

12   Compressed vocal that sounds "squeezed"

13   Compression release setting too quick

14   Compressed vocal by itself (compare to #11)

15   Small vocal sound

16   Small vocal sound in a mix

17   Small vocal sound made into a big sound by compression

18   Same as #17, but in a mix

19   Heavily compressed example with "squeezing" sound

20   Same as #19, but using a sidechain to remove the "squeezing" sound

Equalization

21   10KHz, 1000Hz, 100Hz tones

22   Vocal track with no EQ

23   Vocal track with EQ (150Hz +10dB)

24   Vocal track with EQ (150Hz -10dB)

25   Vocal track with EQ (800Hz +10dB)

26   Vocal track with EQ (800Hz -10dB)

27   Vocal track with EQ (3kHz +10dB)

28   Vocal track with EQ (3kHz -10dB)

29   Vocal track with EQ (10kHz +10dB)

30   Vocal track with EQ (10kHz -10dB)

31   Vocal track with EQ (20kHz +10dB)

32   Vocal example switching into "radio" voice with EQ

Tracking Vocals

33   Obvious (bad) punch-ins on a vocal

34   Discrete (good) punch-ins on a vocal

35   Seamless punch-in (at the beginning of a word)

36   Weak vocal line in music that could use doubling

37   Same as #36, but with the vocal doubled

38   Music example with one lead vocal line

39   Music example with one lead and one overpowering background voice

40   Same as #39, but with an EQ on the backgrounds to help them blend

41   Music example with one weak background part

42   Same as #41, but with the part tripled in order to make it fuller

Reverb

43   Dry vocal line (no effects)

44   Same as #43, but with a room reverb

45   Only the room reverb from #44 (dry vocal removed)

46   Music example with dry vocal

47   Same as #46, but with a room reverb on vocal

48   Same as #43, but with a hall reverb

49   Only the hall reverb from #48 (dry vocal removed)

50   Same as #43, but with a plate reverb

51   Only the plate reverb from #50 (dry vocal removed)

52   Music example with plate reverb on the vocal

53   Vocal with standard plate reverb setting (decay = 2.36 seconds)

54   Same as #53, but with modified decay time (decay = 1.07 seconds)

55   Vocal with standard room reverb setting

56   Same as #55, but with HFC setting at 4kHz

57   Reverb example with no predelay

58   Same as #57, but with an 80ms predelay setting

Delay

59 Same as #43, but with 300ms delay

60 Music example with delay on the vocal
    (310ms with a 10% feedback setting)

61 Delay effect (2 repeats with a 3% feedback
    setting)

62 Delay effect with 15% setting for feedback

63 Vocal panned left and right (appears in the
    center)

64 Same as #63, but with a 40ms delay on the
    right side

65 Music example using stereo delay (32ms, 0%
    feedback)

66 Delay/reverb effect

67 Music example using delay/reverb effect

Chorus

68 Chorus effect example

69 Chorus example with too much depth
    (100% setting)

70 Chorus example with too little depth
    (3% setting)

71 Music example using chorus effect

Noise Gate

72 Noisy vocal track (needs gating)

73 Same as #72, but with a gate to get rid of the
    noise

74 Gate example with a threshold setting that is
    too low

75 Gate example with a threshold setting that is
    too high

76 Gate example with a range setting that is too
    low

77 Gate example with a release setting that is
    short

78 Gate example with a release setting that is
    long

Auto-Tuner

79 Music example with a vocal that is slightly off
    pitch

80 Same as #79, but with the Antares auto-tune
    3.0 on the vocal

Answers to Quiz Questions

CD examples for TRACK 1-3:

     Track 1: Shure condenser microphone

     Track 2: Shure dynamic microphone

     Track 3: Neumann condenser microphone

Shure condenser, Shure dynamic, Neumann condenser

CD example (of punch-ins) for TRACK 34:

(punch) I wish I told you *(punch)* these words long ago. *(punch)* I'm reminded of wasted breath *(punch)* and all the tears *(punch)* that have now gone cold.

CD example for TRACK 62 (15% feedback setting):

4 complete repeats after the initial dry vocal

Musicians Institute Press

is the official series of Southern California's renowned music school, Musicians Institute. **MI** instructors, some of the finest musicians in the world, share their vast knowledge and experience with you – no matter what your current level. For guitar, bass, drums, vocals, and keyboards, **MI Press** offers the finest music curriculum for higher learning through a variety of series:

ESSENTIAL CONCEPTS
Designed from MI core curriculum programs.

MASTER CLASS
Designed from MI elective courses.

PRIVATE LESSONS
Tackle a variety of topics "one-on-one" with MI faculty instructors.

KEYBOARD

Funk Keyboards – The Complete Method
A Contemporary Guide to Chords, Rhythms, and Licks
by Gail Johnson • **Master Class**
00695336 Book/CD Pack $14.95

Jazz Hanon
by Peter Deneff • **Private Lessons**
00695554 . . . . $12.95

Keyboard Technique
by Steve Weingard • **Essential Concepts**
00695365 . . . . $12.95

Keyboard Voicings: The Complete Guide
by Kevin King • **Essential Concepts**
00695209 . . . . $12.95

Music Reading for Keyboard
by Larry Steelman • **Essential Concepts**
00695205 . . . . $12.95

R&B Soul Keyboards
by Henry J. Brewer • **Private Lessons**
00695327 Book/CD Pack $16.95

Salsa Hanon
by Peter Deneff • **Private Lessons**
00695226 . . . . $12.95

DRUM

Afro-Cuban Coordination for Drumset
by Maria Martinez • **Private Lessons**
00695328 Book/CD Pack $14.95

Blues Drumming
By Ed Roscetti • **Essential Concepts**
00695623 Book/CD Pack $14.95

Brazilian Coordination for Drumset
by Maria Martinez • **Master Class**
00695284 Book/CD Pack $14.95

Chart Reading Workbook for Drummers
by Bobby Gabriele • **Private Lessons**
00695129 Book/CD Pack $14.95

Drummer's Guide to Odd Meters
by Ed Roscehi • **Essential Concepts**
00695349 Book/CD Pack $14.95

Latin Soloing for Drumset
by Phil Maturano • **Private Lessons**
00695287 Book/CD Pack $14.95

Working the Inner Clock for Drumset
by Phil Maturano • **Private Lessons**
00695127 Book/CD Pack $16.95

VOICE

Harmony Vocals: The Essential Guide
by Mike Campbell & Tracee Lewis • **Private Lessons**
00695262 Book/CD Pack $17.95

Sightsinging
by Mike Campbell • **Essential Concepts**
00695195 . . . . $17.95

Vocal Technique
By Dena Murray • **Master Class**
00695427 Book/CD Pack $19.95

ALL INSTRUMENTS

An Approach to Jazz Improvisation
by Dave Pozzi • **Private Lessons**
00695135 Book/CD Pack $17.95

Encyclopedia of Reading Rhythms
by Gary Hess • **Private Lessons**
00695145 . . . . $19.95

Going Pro
by Kenny Kerner • **Private Lessons**
00695322 . . . . $17.95

Home Recording Basics Featuring Dallan Beck
00695655 Video $19.95

Harmony & Theory
by Keith Wyatt & Carl Schroeder • **Essential Concepts**
00695161 . . . . $17.95

Lead Sheet Bible
by Robin Randall • **Private Lessons**
00695130 Book/CD Pack $19.95

WORKSHOP SERIES

Transcribed scores of the greatest songs ever!

Blues Workshop
00695137 . . . . $22.95

Classic Rock Workshop
00695136 . . . . $19.95

AUDIO
TECHNOLOGY BOOKS

FROM HAL LEONARD

Mackie Compact Mixers – 2nd Edition

Now in its expanded and updated second edition, Mackie Compact Mixers takes the mystery out of using your mixer. Written in a clear, musician-friendly style, this book will help you get the most from your small mixer, whatever its brand or model. Provides specific information and hook-up examples on Mackie's most popular models, including the "classic" 1202 and 1604 as well as the new 1202-, 1402-, 1604-VLZs, VLZ Pro and other models. Written by the author of Live Sound for Musicians and authorized by Mackie, this book explains the fundamental concepts of how mixing boards work, emphasizing how audio gets into and out of a mixer. Armed with this understanding of signal flow, you will be equipped to begin answering your own questions about how to set up and operate your mixer to best meet your needs.

00330477..$27.95

The Recording Guitarist

A Guide for Home and Studio by Jon Chappell

This is a practical, hands-on guide to a variety of recording environments, from modest home studios – where the guitarist must also act as the engineer and producer – to professional facilities outfitted with top-quality gear and staffed with audio engineers. This book will prepare guitarists for any recording situation and will help them become familiar with all facets of recording technology and procedure. Topics covered include: guitars and amps for recording; effects; mixer logic and routing strategies; synching music to moving images; and how to look and sound professional, with advice from Alex Lifeson, Carl Verheyen, Steve Lukather, Eric Johnson and others. Also includes complete info on the classic set-ups of 14 guitar greats, from Hendrix to Vai.

00330335..$19.95

Audio Made Easy – 2nd Edition

Audio Made Easy is a book about professional audio written in terms that everyone can understand. Chapters include info on mixers, microphones, amplifiers, speakers and how they all work together. New edition features a new section on wireless mics. New edition features a new section on wireless mics.

00330260..$12.95

Yamaha Guide to Sound Systems for Worship

The Yamaha Guide to Sound Systems for Worship is written to assist in the design, purchase, and operation of a sound system. It provides the basic information on sound systems that is most needed by ministers, members of Boards of Trustees and worship and music committees, interested members of congregations, and even employees of musical instrument dealers that sell sound systems. To be of greatest value to all, it is written to be both nondenominational and "non-brand-name."

00290243..$24.95

Live Sound for Musicians

Finally, a live sound book written for musicians, not engineers! Live Sound for Musicians tells you everything you need to know to keep your band's PA system working smoothly, from set-up to sound check right through performance. Author Rudy Trubitt give you all the information you need, and leaves out the unnecessary propeller-head details that would just slow you down. So if you're the player in the band who sets up the PA, this is the book you've been waiting for!

00330249..$19.95

Sound Check – The Basics of Sound and Sound Systems

Sound Check is a simplified guide to what can be a tricky subject: getting good sound. Starting with an easy-to-understand explanation of the principles and physics of sound, Sound Check goes on to cover amplifiers, speaker hookup, matching speakers with amps, sound reinforcement, mixers, monitor systems, grounding, and more.

00330118..$14.95

Yamaha Sound Reinforcement Handbook – 2nd Edition

Sound reinforcement is the use of audio amplification systems. This book is the first and only book of its kind to cover all aspects of designing and using such systems for public address and musical performance. The book features information on both the audio theory involved and the practical applications of that theory, explaining everything from microphones to loud speakers. This revised edition features almost 40 new pages and is even easier to follow with the addition of an index and a simplified page and chapter numbering system. New topics covered include: MIDI, synchronization, and an appendix on logarithms.

00500964..$34.95